"Erik Seversen has consciously [ ] tions throughout life, the stories ˍˌ .... book Explore. Reading this book will not only transport you to the Amazon Jungle and the Alaskan Wilderness, but to the very center of your search to live life on your own terms. I'm inspired to check off more items on my bucket list, to be a better human, and to experience all that life promises us (but doesn't guarantee)."

—ADAM CARROLL, Author of
The Build a Bigger Life Manifesto

"With his unique storytelling skills, Erik Seversen pulls you into his world, like you are sitting right there alongside him. His riveting stories open your eyes to the beauty of becoming better even in the worst of situations. Life is growth and this book places the importance of growth and love back where they belong, at the center of our lives. As a national educator and speaker, I certainly recommend this book to enhance your own ability to extract life's gems of living a creative and courageous life."

—GENEIN LETFORD, M.Ed., Bestselling author of
Debt to Destiny: Creating Financial Freedom from the Inside Out

"Erik's life journey opens up a life of adventure. It's not a book you will be able to put down once you have started, and the stories will most likely never be forgotten after you've read them. His adaptability to culture creates a platform for him to understand who he is on a more insightful level. When you interact with his journey, it allows you to dive deeper into who you are. The questions that are mapped at the ending of each chapter help as well. Regarding the first story, Erik, who lets a shaman touch you that way?"

—ENGEL JONES, Host of 12-minute Convos podcast
and author of Y.O.U.R.S: Your Own Unique Real Self

"In Explore, Erik Seversen takes us on fantastic adventures through his personal life stories, but the book also forces the reader to question meaning in a way that shows that happiness and success are not goals to be reached, but they are available while spending time with family, snowboarding down a mountain, or while teaching customer service training. After reading Explore, you will see happiness and success in a new light."

—DAVID BROWNLEE, CEO of Pure Customer Service and bestselling author of *Rockstar Service Rockstar Profits*

"In this uniquely written book, Erik shares his personal life stories so the reader can engage and reflect on their life. But more than that, he gets us to consider insights and applications for our own lives. Enjoy – you will appreciate the power that stories can and will have on others."

—KEN KEIS, Ph.D., Bestselling author of *Why Aren't You More Like Me?*

"Erik is an outstanding storyteller. He describes events in such a way that brings the reader into the story as a fellow voyager. This book, however, goes beyond those descriptions. Each episode is followed by thought and action-provoking questions that challenge the reader to go "beyond extraordinary" in their own lives. In the arena of love, you are challenged to step outside yourself. In the area of personal growth, you are asked to go beyond the familiar. Erik asks you to view happiness as a choice. In that you find success. Explore *invites you to live on the edge and by doing so discover who you are and where you are going."*

—BEN ERICKSON, Author of *Tell Them They Are Chosen*

EXPLORE.

EXPLORE.

EXTRAORDINARY ADVENTURES OF VULNERABILITY AND STRENGTH

ERIK SEVERSEN

THIN LEAF PRESS | LOS ANGELES

Disclaimer—some names and identifying details have been changed to protect the privacy of individuals.

Library of Congress Cataloging-in-Publication Data
Names: Seversen, Erik, Author

Title: Explore. Extraordinary Adventures of Vulnerability and Strength

LCCN 2020909407
ISBN 978-1-7323369-3-3 | ISBN 978-1-7323369-2-6 (eBook)
Memoir, Travel Narrative, Self-Development
Cover Design: 100 Covers
Interior Design: Formatted Books
Editor: Nancy Pile
Copy Editor: Rebecca Lau
Thin Leaf Press
Los Angeles

THIN
LEAF

Thank you for reading this book. I wrote *Explore* to be about you as much as it is about me. If you like what you see and would like to connect with me beyond just the words within these pages, please reach out to me directly—Erik@ErikSeversen.com

If you are the type of person who likes to jump right into things, you should begin the EXTRAORDINARY HABITS CHALLENGE now. This is a list of simple mental and physical habits that, when implemented into your routine, will greatly increase your energy, productivity, and sense of fulfillment. Enact these habits today, so you can find or further develop *extraordinary* success in your life.

You can find the challenge at www.ErikSeversen.com.

To Diep, Jack, and Ben who keep life wonderful
and keep me inspired.

CONTENTS

PREFACE

I was climbing first, with nothing but my ice axe and the points of my crampons holding me to the frozen wall. Below was a thousand feet of nothing. My body pulsed as I slowly worked my way up, relying on experience and focus. We'd made a conscious decision not to rope up. Above us was nearly vertical hard ice, and we'd decided that if one of us were to fall, the other two couldn't arrest his fall.

We were near the summit of the mountain. I'd planned to get through this section and place an ice anchor from which to belay Glen and Carl, my climbing partners, but they were climbing up behind me, un-roped. Once we all made the summit, we hugged and cheered our success. We were celebrating not only reaching the summit of the mountain, we were celebrating life on the edge.

In the case of the mountain climb, the edge was real. It was a physical edge from which we could fall. But "the edge" is also a metaphor for living beyond the boundaries of the normal, beyond comfort, beyond the familiar, and beyond the safe boundaries of ordinary. The edge is a place of exploration, and the edge is the place where I have chosen to live my life.

My previous book, *Ordinary to Extraordinary*, contained narratives showing how belonging, purpose, transcendence, and storytelling each contributed to my finding meaning in my life and how those pillars can bolster you in your pursuit of a meaningful life as well. Based on concepts from Emily Esfahani Smith's book, *The Power of Meaning*, in this previous book I related how living with the Wayana Indians in the Amazon helped me gain a sense of belonging; how walking through Africa gave me a sense of purpose; how experiencing the aurora borealis created in me a transcendental moment; and how writing a book completed, for me, Esfahani Smith's four pillars of meaning by allowing me to share my story.

Ordinary to Extraordinary, however, was written to be more than about me. My adventures are actually the least important part of the book; rather, it's how my story provokes thoughts, decisions, and action in you regarding your own relationship with meaning. That's where the magic happens. The book you are holding now acts as an extension of that same idea. Like *Ordinary to Extraordinary*, this book is composed of moments from my life that could very well spark in you a glimpse of the palpable satisfaction that choosing to live on the edge, beyond the ordinary, allows. *Explore* is also about what I learned from my experiences. Experiences such as taking hallucinogenic drugs with Indians in the Amazon, unexpectedly having to fight a bouncer at a bowling alley, falling in love with a woman whom I'd never see again, and crashing a Harley-Davidson on Hollywood Boulevard.

Admittedly in some of these stories, you'll see that I was sometimes foolish, sometimes made risky choices, and even at times put my life and the lives of others in danger. I wouldn't change my past, but I'm not proud of these particular moments either, and I thank God that He was looking out for me. There are many times when I should have "gone over the edge," meeting tragedy or death, but I didn't. And that's the thing about the edge—it accelerates not just your life experience but also your growth as a person. I like to think that the edge necessarily grows our levels of wisdom and compassion, even when we escape falling off that edge by the seat of our pants.

I hope that while reading this book, you are encouraged not to remain in the comfortable center where average thrives, but that you'll push yourself to move toward the edge, beyond ordinary, and all the while carefully maintaining that line between exhilaration and danger.

I should add that the edge doesn't have to be a dangerous place. Yes, there is an edge while speeding along on a motorcycle that equates to physical death, but there are many kinds of places we call *the edge*. There is the edge of learning, where we explore unknown things even within our own brains. There is the edge of romance where we become vulnerable to rejection and hurt. Whatever your edge may be, the edge is a place of being alive, of feeling the intensity of your choices and your actions. The edge is the place where you look at things larger than yourself and experience wonder. And gratitude.

So, come with me now and enjoy the following pages. I invite you to immerse yourself into these stories from a life lived beyond the ordinary and beyond the extraordinary. Hopefully, you'll be inspired to step out and explore the edge in your own life.

Continuing to draw from Emily Esfahani Smith's book, *The Power of Meaning*, I've grouped the following narratives into two sections, "Love" and "Growth." With a short commentary about love—which also encompasses friendship—and growth—implying continued learning—at the end of each section as well as personal questions for you to answer at the end of each chapter. I hope you are challenged to look at your own past, present, and future to reflect on your life. Who are you? Where are you going? And, what does the edge mean to you? Equipped with these questions and your current answers, there is nothing you can't do while living a meaningful life filled with happiness, success, and wonder.

PART 1

LOVE

Love is the ultimate and the highest goal to which man can aspire.

—Viktor Frankl

ONE

YALUWA-OKOI AND THE WAYANA

French Guiana, South America. 1995. Twenty-Six Years Old

I was near the coast in French Guiana across the river from Suriname. I wanted to get upriver into the forest area inhabited by the Wayana Indians. I was an undergrad at UCLA, and I'd been awarded a research grant, but it didn't come with instructions on how to get into the jungle. So that's what I was figuring out.

I tried to get passage with one of the Aluku, a Maroon Tribe. They were known to transport supplies upriver to an outpost city called Maripasoula, which is about seven days' travel up the remote river, in very large dugout canoes with outboard motors attached to the back. I couldn't find anyone heading upriver in St. Laurent, the only city I knew of on the Maroni. I finally figured out that I had to go to an Aluku enclave just south of the small city, but even when I found a transport canoe departing the following morning, they didn't want to take me. The reason was partially because they thought it would be an inconvenience, but mostly because the Aluku are a very reserved, almost secretive tribe with a heightened sense of caution for all outsiders.

Finally, the next morning, after many attempts to get on the boat, I decided to try another tactic. I negotiated the cost of five 50-pound sacks of potatoes, which I said I wanted transported to Maripasoula. The price was set, I handed over the money, and then I—rather than 250 pounds of potatoes—stepped into the mostly loaded pirogue.

The canoe driver protested, but I explained that the negotiated 250 pounds was more weight than me and my pack together and that I had all my own food with me.

In the end, he accepted, and he was glad he did. I ended up unloading supplies at various Aluku villages along the river for him over the next seven days. Not only that, but anytime the river became wide and too shallow, or had a *soula* or forceful rapid, we had to unload the entire pirogue, get the canoe past the area, carry the supplies around, and reload it all. I knew I didn't have to, but I like to be helpful, and, besides, there was nothing else to do.

I was also able to get to know many people in tiny villages whom I would have otherwise never had a chance to meet. The seven-day trip to Maripasoula worked out to be a good way to ease my way into the three months I'd spend in the jungle. I became good friends with Bakos and Naipon, who were leading the voyage.

***

Three years later, as a graduate student at University of Virginia, when I needed to get upriver for further research, it was easy. I found Bakos right away, and he got me on a canoe with one of his friends. The trip upriver was much like the one I had done before, and it was good to see some of the same villagers as on the previous trip. This time, however, I was going further upriver past Maripasoula to conduct research among the Wayana Indians. I had originally planned to research the unique relationship between the Wayana Amerindians and the Aluku Maroons, a tribe with African origins who have lived in the Americas for generations, but I ended up focusing on something entirely different.

Getting to Maripasoula wasn't a problem, but I had no idea how I would get further upriver into Wayana territory. The closer I got to Maripasoula, the more concerned I became. Since I had already spent quite a bit of time in Maripasoula on my earlier trip working with the Aluku, I knew the large village quite well. Maripasoula had a school, a French police outpost, and a small infirmary with a French doctor and one nurse.

As soon as I arrived, I made my rounds. It was great to get back to the calm village, and I marveled at the traditional A-frame huts on the north side of the village and the colorful Aluku paintings on doorways and on canoes. The infirmary was the last place I stopped, and the doctor told me that once a month he traveled upriver to provide medical assistance to the Amerindians. To my luck, he was scheduled to leave the very next day. He said that I could sleep on the couch of the infirmary, and we'd leave at dawn the following morning. Going on the trip would be the doctor, his large medical kit, a Wayana named Amaca, and me.

The doctor was excited to speak with someone from outside of the small, remote community in which he'd been living for six months, so we celebrated the good timing of my arrival with a few mixed drinks of white rum, lime, and sugar. We had wonderful conversations getting to know each other and called it an early night in preparation for the long trip.

Maripasoula also acts as the governmental boundary restricting outsiders from entering Wayana territory. The restriction is to help protect the Wayana and a few other indigenous groups who lived upriver from exploitation as well as disease. I had permission to enter for research, and before we left, the doctor made sure the gendarme checked my papers as he checked my lengthy vaccination card.

"All good," Jacques, the doctor, said to me as he folded up the yellow booklet and handed it back. Jacques also gave me a bit of cultural information about the Wayana and explained a few things that I should expect.

I knew very little about the Wayana, and I really didn't have any plans on exactly what I was going to do or where I was going to stay. One guy had written a bit about the Wayana in French, but I was essentially going in with nothing other than a research thesis, which was important to the University of Virginia, but which meant nothing to the Indians with whom I wanted to live. I was apprehensive as we moved upriver.

We ended up stopping at three small villages, one each day, before arriving at Dakoye, which was as far as Jacques was traveling, and the village at which Jacques had hoped I would be able to stay.

As we neared the village, Jacques said that I was in luck. There was a *ta'akai* going on in Dakoye. A *ta'akai* is basically a ceremonial celebration among the Wayana. It takes weeks to build up to these gatherings, but ultimately, they are drink-fests in which one village will invite neighboring villages, and the party lasts until all the *cashiri* is gone. I would learn later the social significance of these gatherings, but at this point, for me it was just a big party of drinking *cashiri*, which is a mildly alcoholic brew made from manioc, also known as cassava. Basically, the women in the village chew up small chunks of manioc, spit it into wooden vats where it ferments over a period of weeks. When the *cashiri* is ready, others are invited, and the *ta'akai* begins. It usually takes between two and three days for the *cashiri* to run out, and that is when the event is over.

I entered Dakoye on the second day of the *ta'akai*. Jacques said that it would be good for me because I could meet everyone in the village all at once, but it would be difficult for him to do his work because most of the Wayana had been drinking their native brew for over 24 hours.

When we pulled the dugout canoe up to the bank in front of Dakoye, not all the villagers ran down to meet us as had happened at the other villages we'd visited over the past few days. We got out and walked up toward the central communal shelter where most of the people were gathered. It was nothing more than a large, wall-less expanse of dirt floor with rough benches along the edges and a thatched roof. Some people were dancing, many were sitting and talking, and the kids were running around playing with bows and arrows.

As I looked around, I saw an older man notice us. He walked toward us with a large gourd full with a thick, milky liquid, which I would soon learn was *cashiri*. He immediately held it out to the doctor who accepted the gourd, drank the entire thing, and said, "*Ipoc moni*" or "Thank you."

Another man came up with a large vessel of *cashiri*. The older man dipped the gourd in, filling it, and he held this one up for me. I looked at the doctor and asked with my eyes if I should drink a sip or all of it. He knew what I was asking, and he twisted his hands up indicating that I should down the whole thing, which I did.

"*Ipoc moni*," I said, copying Jacques.

The old man smiled, and Jacques told me that he was the chief of the Wayana. The doctor then asked Amaca, who spoke both French and Wayana, to ask the chief if it would be okay if I stayed in the village.

The chief quickly responded that it would be okay, and the guy who had come with him smiled and told Amaca that I could stay in his hut with his family. As the doctor gathered his medical kit and set up a workstation, where a line of women and children was quickly forming, the man and I went to the canoe, retrieved my belongings, and hung my hammock in his small, wall-less hut.

And then the party started ...

As soon as my hammock was hung, the man named Yagu, walked me around to introduce me to others in the village. A few of the Indians in this village spoke a bit of French, but it really didn't seem to matter that we couldn't communicate very well at all. Most of the men who lived in the village had a container of *cashiri* next to them, and they'd offer me a gourd full each time we met. I would learn later that I did the right thing in accepting all of the drink offerings, as it would have been culturally very offensive to refuse any. I felt drunk within minutes, and I loved it.

As the day turned to evening, more and more people joined in the rhythmic dance that never ended in the center of the large communal hut, and the drinking of *cashiri* continued. Many times, people would vomit, and later this would be a cultural aspect of the Wayana that I'd write much about.

I became totally buzzed on my first day with the Wayana. I felt like I was best friends with everybody, and finally at about midnight, the *cashiri* was finished. People started falling asleep. When I knew it was time for me to go to bed, I could barely remember where to go, but I found my hammock near the far side of the village, crawled in, and smiled to myself that I had made it. I officially had a place to stay and was accepted into a Wayana village.

My honeymoon in the village didn't last forever, but many very interesting things happened while I stayed in the hut at the far side of Dakoye. The first was the very next day when I woke up, I would learn that there wasn't any private ownership among the Wayana, and that everything was communal. A few items like bows, shotguns, metal pots, and machetes traded upriver were generally left alone and not borrowed, but I learned that boxer shorts did not fall into this category.

When I'd entered the forest, I'd brought seven pairs of boxer shorts with me. I figured this was an obvious number for a week's worth of shorts, but when I woke up the next morning, I saw six young Wayana wearing boxer shorts. They wore them for a few days before tiring of them. I never saw them again, so I was left with the one pair I was wearing.

My whole pack had been searched through before I was awake, but my knife, camera, and everything else was untouched. I wasn't concerned at all. They weren't trying to steal anything since, as Jacques had warned me, personal property really wasn't a big deal to them.

***

By far, the strangest thing that happened while I was staying in the hut occurred about three weeks after I'd arrived. It started when a group of Wayana men formed around an individual who was on his knees gathering a concoction of plants into a twisted cone. The men were all hovering in anticipation, and when the Wayana at the center of the group lit the concoction, there was a murmur. Everyone ceremoniously sat in a circle, and the lit concoction moved from one person to the next. It was less about peer pressure than about anthropological curiosity for me to join them when the concoction wrapped in a thin section of a dried banana leaf was passed to me.

Should I? I wondered.

A bit tentative about not knowing what it was, I tried not to pull too much of the smoke into my lungs, but it didn't take long before the thin leaves around me became like skinny vipers striking at my legs. All around my calves, shins, and ankles, the thin snakes were striking, and their long venomous fangs were sticking deeply into my flesh. Everywhere I stepped, there were more of the snakes. I found that at this point, the group of Wayana men and I were walking around a large grassy area. Our movements were strange. I couldn't tell if we were playing volleyball or searching for something.

At times, one or more of the men would look at me. At times, everyone was simultaneously staring at me. Sometimes there were smiles of encouragement, and other times there was laughter. I realized that I was becoming nervous in this unfamiliar place. Worse. I became paranoid, and I was bringing down the rest of the group. They didn't like it. I felt like I was ruining the collective consciousness that we were sharing.

What did I get myself into? Was I imagining this?

There was one Yanomamo who was living in the Wayana village. He had two wives because he was such a good hunter. We had become "friends" earlier on a multi-day hunting trip, but without a common word between us. Our friendship was him slapping mosquitoes off me when they landed on me while sitting around a fire one night, and I'd do the same for him. He was unique. His hunting ability was superlative. I'd seen him shoot an arrow into a tree, jump from the canoe, climb 20 feet up to grab a large angry monkey stuck to his long, barbed arrow, and bring it down in seconds with the grace of an acrobat.

In this moment, however, I was petrified of him. He was a Yanomamo, from the famed tribe named the "Fierce People" who are known to be skeptical of outsiders and who express violence almost for sport. He was always intense, and I knew that I was bringing down the collective energy of our communal vision, and I sensed that he was getting angry.

He'll come after me any moment, I thought to myself, becoming more and more paralyzed with fear. He did not attack, but he knew what I was thinking. I felt like I had to get out of this situation. I might have mumbled something to some of the men in the grassy area, but I basically just walked out of the scene. They looked at me in disbelief, but I crossed the village and crawled into my hammock.

Lying frightened in my hammock, I looked out of the wall-less hut and could see the chief of the Emerillon sitting outside his tiny hut. This was not normal. The village of Dakoye was made up of two parts. On one side, the larger side of the village, were the Wayana, but there were also a small group of Emerillon Indians living in one section of the village. The elderly Emerillon chief was always inside his small enclosed hut at dusk every night for three weeks straight. But on this night, he was not only outside, he was sitting on the ground next to a small fire, facing my direction. He was looking at me, and it was as if he were calling me. I didn't know what to do. I thought something paranormal was happening, and I couldn't ignore it.

I got out of my hammock, picked up two cigarettes, and walked over to the Emerillon chief. He motioned for me to sit across the fire from him, and he also turned, so that he was facing the fire and toward me. He sat there with his long hair hanging down both sides of his wrinkled, tan face, and he stared at me. I lit a cigarette and handed it to him. I lit a cigarette for myself ...

I have absolutely no memory of what happened after that and for the following number of minutes. My next memory is of the chief sucking on the finished cigarette as a tiny bit of the butt of the cigarette burned near his lips. He looked at me intently and nodded that I was finished. I felt like he had said something to me or had somehow given me something, but I had no idea what it was. As I walked back to my hut, the chief disappeared into his shelter.

When I got back to my hammock, I could hear singing in the Wayana village. Many people were involved in the singing. It was the first time I'd heard this type of singing in the village. It felt distant, but right next to me as well. At times the singing was beautiful and harmonic, and at other times it sounded like sickening and frightening screams.

The stillness in my hammock was too overwhelming, so I got out, sat on a stool, and began writing about the experience in my journal in an attempt at controlling what was happening. I had just started writing when a very elderly woman started slowly walking toward my hut. The owner of the hut and his family were away visiting another village, and I was alone.

As the woman approached, I could see that she was carrying a rattle in one hand, and she was also carrying a baby who was trying to suckle her breast, which was absolutely dry and unproductive, almost like a large flap of skin hanging in the direction of the ground. The old woman was humming or chanting, as she systematically walked, shaking the rattle along the perimeter of my hut only feet away from me. I stopped writing and just looked at her. I was vaguely aware that the viper-like grass earlier was a hallucination, but that this was happening, and I didn't know why. It seemed as if she were setting up some sort of protective barrier around my hut.

As soon as the woman had walked with the ornamented shaker along the entire perimeter of my hut, the chief of the Wayana walked over and sat next to me. He had never done this before. I had one cigarette left, so I lit it and gave it to him. He just sat next to me, and my body buzzed with a nervous energy. The chief didn't say anything, but he sat next to me for about five minutes. Then he looked at me and said, "*Attends*," which is French for "Wait." He said this twice and then walked away.

I sat doing nothing for a long number of minutes. A group of three Wayana boys about seven or eight years old came over and started looking at my journal. I gave them my pencil, and they drew pictures for a few minutes and then went away. Somehow, I thought that that was what I was supposed to wait for. I wasn't entirely comfortable because of my reaction to the drug, and my nervousness was still on high.

Again, I couldn't stand doing nothing, so I began to write. Next, it was as if my pencil took control, and I wrote some random things ending in, *"Since you are writing, I won't come."*

As soon as I looked down at the paper and saw this, I was even more frightened. I became trumped by confusion and my inability to hold on to a thought. I didn't know what the writing meant or where it had come from. I stopped writing, crawled into my hammock, and desperately prayed for sleep.

Finding sleep took a very long time because I was having visions. The visions were of faces, but not human faces, rather animals. The first was a jaguar, then a large boa constrictor, an owl, a hummingbird, and many more, but it ended with the sustaining image of the head of an eagle staring directly into my face from a few inches away. The vision wasn't in color but in shades from almost pale-like white to black, and the eagle just stared and stared until I finally drifted off.

The next morning, I woke up early feeling great, but I was also pensive about the prior evening. To this day, I have no idea what was going on, but it was definitely something inimitable.

I got out of my hammock, walked down a small grassy path to a tiny branch off the river, and bathed in the cool, clear water. Just as I returned to my hut, one of the Wayana men came over. He was with a shaman. He had a tattoo on his chest and a few paintings on his arm.

After introductions, the shaman asked if I was a good singer. He looked dejected when I said that I wasn't. I'm not sure what initiated this, but the Wayana who had brought the shaman over asked me to tell him about what had happened the evening before.

I told him about the experience, and I didn't leave out the part about how paranoid I had become. I would have loved it if the shaman would have explained his interpretation of what had happened, but he simply reached down and grabbed my penis and held it softly in his fingertips for a few seconds. While he was doing this, it looked like he was thinking, as a mathematician trying to figure out an equation in his head. He then simply let go and took a dried banana-leaf cigarette out of the bag he was carrying and lit it.

"Smoke this instead," he said to me as he handed me the rolled banana leaf. I took one puff, and instantly knew that it was filled only with tobacco. It did give me a massive head rush, but nothing compared to what had happened the night before. I kept the natural cigarette, but never felt compelled to light it again. I did have a few more intense drug-induced journeys with the Indians, which continue to challenge my understanding of reality when I try to rationalize them.

***

After about a month staying in the hut of Yagu, his wife, and their one young child, everything changed. I was gathering a few things near my hammock when Yagu started talking with me in Wayana. I couldn't understand a thing, and then he became more and more agitated. He began yelling.

I cautiously backed up, as he was waving his hands up and down, excitedly screaming. I had absolutely no idea what was happening, but because I could see it escalating, I was getting ready to defend myself for when he might attack. He looked like he was getting out of control, and the yelling and stomping of his feet continued.

This went on for a few minutes, and then Alaywe, one of the young Wayana men whom I had gone hunting with quite a few times, walked across the small village. He didn't say a word, but he very calmly untied my hammock from Yagu's hut, grabbed my hand, and walked me across the center of the village to his family's compound. This was a much larger series of huts where he, his wife's parents, and his brother and sister lived. He let go of my hand and hung my hammock there. As soon as he did this, he said, "Yaluwa-okoi can live here."

I didn't know it at the time, but that was when I was "officially" adopted as a Wayana. As soon as Alaywe did this, his sister started referring to me as "spouse," and his brother started calling me "brother." I finally fit in with the kinship structure of the village and was actually part of it. Once we were away from Yagu, Alaywe explained that Yagu was getting more and more angry that I hadn't been contributing enough meat for the family, but that I would eat meat almost every day.

It is certainly true that I wasn't as good of a hunter as the rest of the Wayana, and I'd less frequently brought back hunted meat than Yagu, but I had contributed. During many meals, I'd very intentionally eaten much less than anyone else, but Yagu had gotten fed up, so I was removed from the situation. It was my scant eating of meat that contributed to my new Wayana name. I think the name "Yaluwa-okoi" meant "man snake" because I was generally a bit bigger and taller than most of the Wayana, but I had become so skinny that my ribs were sticking out under my skin, and, according to Alaywe, it looked funny, so there it was.

***

I was very excited that I had a new name, and it wasn't long after that when Dakoye was invited to another village a few hours away for a *ta'akai*. As we always did when we traveled, we collected up some food to eat in the canoe, gathered our hammocks, and started off.

The beginning of the *ta'akai* was great. On the second day, when everyone was feeling the effects of not eating and only drinking for over a day straight, the barf competitions began. The stomach would become so full of the pulpy liquid *cashiri* that it would become almost impossible to add more into the body.

As I learned among the Wayana, there are three obligations in the culture: an obligation to give, an obligation to receive, and an obligation to reciprocate. This was a fundamental part of Wayana social structure and really kept social relationships strong, but there existed an "escape" from the obligation to reciprocate. This was symbolized by accepting and drinking a gourd full of *cashiri* and immediately reversing the natural process of digestion (and metaphorically "things") and laying the gift out on the ground as a way of saying, "The giving has become too much, so I received the gift from you, but I am not indebted to you; we are still equal."

Along with body adornment and exchange, ritual vomiting became a focus of my anthropology research as I identified the structural significance of the custom of Wayana vomit, but it was much more fun to just be in a line with Wayana men, accepting gourds full of *cashiri* from each other, and then vaulting the liquid in the form of projectile vomit as far as we could and jubilantly congratulating the one who puked the farthest. It was a blast as well as a lot of laughs.

Not all was fun on this particular day, though. There was one Wayana from another village whom I had never seen before, and he kept staring at me. He had been drinking as much *cashiri* as everyone else, but he didn't seem to be enjoying himself in the same way. Then, he started making aggressive movements towards me. The other men in the village intervened within seconds and began yelling at him. He simply walked over to the river, got into a small dugout canoe, and paddled away.

"It is a good thing you are named, Yaluwa-okoi," Alaywe said to me in French.

"Why?" I responded, a bit shaken up.

"Because he might have tried to kill you if you weren't," Alaywe continued. He explained that the name for "foreigner" in Wayana equated to "non-human," so if this guy hated that I was there, killing me would have been the same as shooting a pesky dog with an arrow. However, since I was at least considered human, he only came at me with his hands.

After Alaywe said this to me, I was more proud of my name than ever. Though I'd soon learn that I still didn't quite know my own name.

Later that evening, the *ta'akai* was in full swing. There were a few young girls of about marrying age in the village. I'd seen one of them before, and she was stunning with her wide face, bright eyes, and jet-black hair cut straight across her forehead. I was standing next to Alaywe on one side of me, and two of the girls were standing on the other side of me. Normally, young Wayana men and women of about marrying age were supposed to ignore each other, but sometimes during the *ta'akai*, this wasn't upheld. Suddenly, the girl I'd seen before, now wearing a beaded turquoise Wayana necklace, said something to Alaywe.

"What did she say?" I anxiously asked Alaywe. He told me that she had asked my name.

Wow, I said to myself, excited that she was asking about me. I looked at her, smiled, and exclaimed very proudly, "Yawali."

The two girls about fell over with laughter. Their bright teeth took over their faces as they giggled uncontrollably. Alaywe was laughing also, so I asked him, "What's so funny?"

"Not *ya-wal-i*," Alaywe said laughing. "It is Ya-luwa-okoi," he continued, pronouncing the end of the word emphatically. Still laughing, he said, "*Ya-wal-i* means 'woman.'"

"Oh," I said, my face turning red with embarrassment. Thankfully, I was rescued by an elderly Wayana man who came over to offer me more *cashiri*.

Returning to Dakoye the next day, we glided along the calm water. I had my bow and arrow lying at the bottom of the dugout canoe, and I was holding my shotgun across my lap as we moved along the river scanning the trees for iguanas. We weren't hungry, but we'd rarely travel without also keeping an eye open for food. The breeze was warm on my face, and I looked up seeing Alaywe relaxed, and his sister and youngest brother dozing off peacefully in the middle of the pirogue. I felt tired from the past few days of the *ta'akai*, but I felt alert as well. I marveled at everything I saw, and I felt at peace.

Your Turn to Explore

Have you ever had to adapt to a different culture (even in your own country)? Where was it, and how did you feel?

What is one culture you'd like to learn more about?

Are there any aspects of your own culture that you'd like to understand more? Do you consider your cultural heritage to be part of who you are?

Do Something Extraordinary: I felt love when I was helped by Alaywe and other Wayana during my time in the Amazon, but we don't have to travel to an exotic place to help others. Next time you see someone who looks like they need help with directions or is confused about something, offer some kind assistance.

TWO

STUPID THINGS ARE FUN

Washington State, USA. 1988. Nineteen Years Old

Kirk and I were pretty much inseparable. Our first meeting was when I was being dragged by my ear by Mr. Carter into Mrs. Stevens' sixth grade classroom on the first day of school. Evidently my reputation as a ruffian preceded me, and Mr. Carter, my originally assigned teacher, wanted nothing to do with me. I can't even remember what set him off on that first day of class. I just remember being pulled through the empty hallway and into Mrs. Stevens' classroom.

I actually listened quite well when teachers reprimanded me, but I think Mr. Carter didn't want to have any competition regarding who the toughest guy in his classroom was. Obviously, it was him, but I still sensed a sort of strange competitive vibe from him. Mr. Carter still had a firm hold of my ear and part of my hair as he shrieked to Mrs. Stevens that he wouldn't have me in his class and that she had to take me.

Mrs. Stevens didn't hesitate in accepting me as her thirty-first pupil even though her class was already overloaded. I had had her in the third grade, and we got along great. She didn't mind that I was slower than the others at learning my multiplication tables, could still barely read, and was a bit gregarious at times. I didn't mind joining her class because I still had a crush on her from the third grade, and I liked that she played Neil Diamond in class from time to time.

As Mr. Carter stormed out of the classroom still agitated, I scanned the room for an empty seat among the shocked and staring students. There was only one. It was on the left side of the very front row with a new kid sitting in the attached desk. I was a bit worked up over being dragged down the hall, but looked over at the new kid and said, "Hi, I'm Erik." He had short dark brown hair and his brown eyes were wide; he looked nervous, but he whispered that he was Kirk. Little did we know that that would be the start of a great friendship. With matching maroon and white Members Only jackets, Kirk, Mike Hansen, and I became a trio through that last year of elementary school.

After drifting different directions in junior high, Kirk and I started hanging out again during our junior year of high school. After graduation, it was Kirk, Dale, and I who became a trio. We did our best to balance the line between being in fun, innocent trouble and real trouble, which we mostly avoided. We never looked for trouble, but we enjoyed some intensity, so found ourselves often skirting trouble. Our friendship was based on intellectualism and stupidity, which seemed to work very well. We even discussed getting "matching" customized license plates for our cars, or in my case, for my parents' big red van, which I drove. The plates were to be: *DUMB, DUMBER,* and *DUMBEST* for Kirk, me, and Dale, in that order, and I think we were even going to spell dumber and dumbest with two "M"s and no "B" because we thought it was more dumb.

The original idea for the license plates came during a fancy cocktail party Dale was invited to up in Bellevue, Washington. Dale was the only one who knew anyone at the party, and it was a slightly older crowd who we learned were trying to act even more sophisticated than they were. Kirk, Dale, and I solved that though.

While I was driving my new ride, a small beat-up Honda Civic, to the event, Dale was in the passenger seat, and Kirk was in the back. I didn't bother turning around when I heard Kirk giggling in the backseat. Little did I know what was happening.

Next—an explosion.

Kirk had decided to take a tiny sip from the bottle of champagne that we were bringing as a gift to the soiree. It had been bouncing around on the floor of the backseat for a half-hour before Kirk decided to take a sip. All he had to do was untwist the coiled wire holding the cork on the shaken-up bottle, and the cork popped like a rocket, bouncing wildly off the car's felt ceiling.

The fountain of shaken-up champagne was like a vertical fire hose. Instinctively, Kirk put his open hand over the top of the spewing bottle. Rather than stopping the overflow, this turned it into a high-pressure sprinkler squirting the gaseous liquid all over Dale, me, and the rest of the car.

Every window from front to back and sides was wet on the inside, and when the high pressure spraying ceased, the bottle was more than half empty. Since this was a fancy cocktail party, we were wearing suits, which we hadn't worn in over a year. Now those suits, as well as the rest of us, were soaked. Laughing about it was all we could do.

As we approached the front door of the million-dollar home with its wide stone facade, Kirk's dress shoes were squeaking because there was so much liquid in them.

Smiling broadly, we pressed the doorbell. It wasn't the host who opened the door, but a 20-year-old dude, acting 30, also wearing a suit. He didn't know what to say. He just stared in a kind of confused shock.

Still smiling, we pushed past him and walked into the large kitchen, which was full of people dressed nicely and sporting tall glasses in their hands. Kirk's shoes continued to squeak, and he held up the mostly empty bottle.

"We're here!" Dale announced loudly to the room full of people, none of whom we knew. "And we brought champagne," he continued in the same loud and confident voice.

That part was obvious since it looked like we had just showered in champagne, and we smelled of it. Even our hair was wet.

All the girls in the room started laughing. Most of the guys still looked confused, but finally joined in the laughter. We cheered the host when he walked into the room.

It seemed that the party had been on the stuffy side before we walked in, but after our ridiculous entry, the event became quite upbeat and enjoyable. This was a trend that seemed to follow us everywhere. Without much effort, we became the impetus that turned the benign into the outrageous.

***

It was on the way to a different party, months later, that Kirk and I ended up doing something else that rattled things up a bit. This was a party in Bellingham, and like the cocktail party, we were invited by one couple and didn't know any others who would be there. Kirk picked me up in his station wagon, which was green with fake wood paneling along the sides and a pimped-out sound system.

As we passed Seattle heading north from Tacoma, Kirk was telling me about the latest book he had finished, *The Autobiography of Benjamin Franklin.* Kirk told me many fascinating things about the man, but one of the things I liked best was when Kirk told me that Franklin would take an "air bath" every day. He'd take off all his clothing, open all the doors and windows of his house, and sit naked and think for an hour. Kirk and I were driving fast through the rain listening to Guns N' Roses when I said, "That's a great idea. I'm going to do that right now." I began to strip off all my clothes except my boxer shorts. Kirk decided to do the same. He even managed not to crash the car while stripping down to his shorts while driving.

It was dark outside and pouring down rain, but we opened all the windows of the station wagon. It was freezing, and the thick rain poured into the car from all directions as we sped along the saturated road with water being kicked up from the tires as well. We turned the volume of the music up to 11, and Kirk pushed the car's accelerator all the way down. We were "flying" up the I-5 at about 90 miles per hour. It probably wasn't the serene meditation that old Benjamin Franklin felt during his air baths, as we were yelling back and forth over the loud music and rain, and playing games like who could hold their hand out the window in the freezing rain longest, but it sure was fun.

When we pulled up to the apartment complex where the party was supposed to be, Kirk dug into the pocket of his wet pants, which were on the floor, looking for the scribbled note with the apartment number on it. He found it: number 142.

I picked up the soaked clothes that were on the floor in a puddle of water and said, "There is no way I'm putting these on."

Kirk agreed, so we just picked up our clothes in a soaking wet wad and walked up to apartment 142. We could hear some music coming from behind the door, so we just opened it and walked in. Almost simultaneously as Kirk and I walked into the room, the couple who had invited us to the party walked out from a hallway with white towels wrapped around them.

The coincidence was too much to deny.

One of the guys in the apartment said, "Good idea." He dropped his pants.

Suddenly the other five people in the room seemed to agree, and all clothes started coming off. Mike and Diane dropped the towels revealing nothing underneath them, and Kirk and I, in our boxer shorts, were suddenly the most dressed people in the room. We looked at each other, now the victims of our own ridiculousness, and off came the wet boxers as well.

The best part about all of this is that there was nothing really weird about what had happened. It was comical and amusing, yes, but nothing odd or kinky.

One of the funniest parts was that since Kirk and I didn't know anyone at the party except the hosts, we went through the standard introductions, handshakes, and polite hugs with no clothes on. We were all still giddy about that fact that no one was dressed, but it all felt strangely normal. Kirk and I joined in drinking beer and wine, sat on the floor playing poker and telling stories and jokes like at any other party.

After we had smoked a few joints, pizza seemed like the most perfect food in the world, so we ordered a few pizzas. Thirty minutes later, the doorbell rang. Diane walked over and opened the door wide, still wearing nothing. Her long blonde hair did nothing to hide any part of her naked body.

The delivery boy looked like he had seen a ghost. All of us in the small apartment were still naked, and he just stood there staring with his mouth open. Finally, Diane asked how much and insisted that he come in. Scared half out of his wits, he did, but stood only a few inches inside the open door while we hunted for money in our clothes that were mostly scattered around the edges of the room. Again, thanks to old Ben Franklin, we certainly spiced up the pizza delivery boy's evening.

The party went late, and almost everyone stayed the whole night. We slept under blankets on couches and on the floor but just as it started, nothing happened that wouldn't have happened at any other "clothed" party. As we began waking up early the next morning and started putting our clothes back on, there was a special bond between the members of the small group who'd shared a fantastic, almost surreal experience in a natural and comfortable manner without ever sensing any depraved intentions from anyone in the collection.

Saying our goodbyes to everyone fully clothed seemed a bit odd. Seeing most of the people at the party dressed for the first time and seeing what type of style they each had was almost distracting.

I decided at that moment to wear nothing other than a white T-shirt and jeans for the next month straight, which would also be my first month of college. In my attempt to be non-defining, however, I obviously was creating a definition, but in either case I found a great group of people that first year of college. Kirk was one of them. We often laughed together about how, other than getting better grades, we really hadn't changed much since our introduction in the sixth grade. To this day, Kirk and I remain great friends. Even while living two states apart, we communicate often.

"Stupid Things Are Fun" is still my second favorite motto. You'll find my favorite motto in a later chapter.

Your Turn to Explore

What is one of the silliest things you've ever done? Who were you with? How did it make you feel?

What are some harmless ways to add a bit of humor or fun to an average day?

Do Something Extraordinary: Sometimes just changing our routines, as Kirk and I did when we entered the Bellingham party with our boxer shorts on, can be the impetus to create a truly unique and alive moment. The next time you go to a party, dinner, or event, wear something absolutely different from expected. Bright red pants, a cool hat, or a random hair style—and do it with confidence and joy.

THREE

CENTRAL AFRICAN GIRL

Central African Republic. 1989. Twenty Years Old

"N'Goundere?"

"Yeah, how many people do you need?"

"We're almost full."

"Good."

Almost full, I thought with a sigh of despair when I saw the cram-packed truck that awaited me halfway across the dirt parking lot that doubled as a vegetable market.

"N'Goundere?"

"Yeah."

"Two thousand CFA for you and 600 for your pack."

"No way, my pack isn't that heavy. Two thousand for me and 200 for my pack."

"Five hundred for the pack."

"I only paid 500 for my pack coming from Maroua." This was a lie, but it didn't seem like it. It just came out of my mouth. I had been through this routine bargaining process many times, and I was just about to yell, *"Dernier prix!"* or "Final price," when the driver settled for 350 Central African Francs.

I handed my pack to one of five young boys who wanted to help tie it on the roof of the truck. After one last look to make sure the pack was not coming down the other side, I climbed in through the back door and sat on the six-inch deep hardwood bench that stuck out from the left side of the truck. A woman wearing a tan and brown shawl climbed in behind me and without a thought placed one of her two children on my lap. While adjusting the infant in her arms, she nudged my hip with hers to squeeze more room for the other people who followed her into the already packed truck. After a friendly smile, the man across from me grabbed my left knee and adjusted it between his legs, so that our knees alternated, creating a more comfortable, or should I say, less painful positioning.

It was not long before the truck slowly began to creep forward in the cool morning air. After gaining some speed, three quick thrusts on the brakes squashed everyone closer to the cab, which allowed the baggage boy to come in off the back bumper and slam the un-shut back doors. I was very tired because of a sleepless night alone in a rented room of a brothel, but I could not sleep now because of the brisk wind that came in through the glassless windows that ran the length of the enclosed truck. Wishing that I had not left my coat in my pack, I lowered my head squinting because of the wind on my face and hugged close to the little girl in my lap as she was my only source of heat. Knowing that I also helped keep her warm, I tried my best to shield her from the cold wind while she slept. Her head was bobbing gently on my chest, leaving little round spots of saliva on my dirty shirt.

After about two hours of this, the sun started to rise above the line of green-leafed trees, and the wind seemed a little more bearable. In fact, I had managed to go into a trance-like sleep. After slowly awakening, I lifted my head, realizing that I too had drooled in my sleep. My eyes stopped on the eyes of another. It was a completely natural exchange. She did not smile, but simply looked. She was beautiful. As I stared, neither of us was embarrassed.

She is an antelope, I thought. *She is an antelope in the most pure, beautiful, and natural sense of the word.*

She was young and thin, crowded between a lady and an elderly man, both of whom were asleep with their heads bobbing to the motion of the dirt road. Her eyes were true brown, blending in with her unnoticeably black pupils. Her skin was of olive quality, dark brown, and smooth in appearance. She had a green and white shawl covering her head, but you could see thin black braids hanging down one side of her face and returning back into her shawl just beneath her ear, which held a small silver hoop. Her face was long and thin, and her lips were brown and full, looking almost as tall as they were wide. She also had a tattoo. One single black line that ran vertically from between her eyebrows halfway up her high forehead.

Oh, what love!

I realized that I was no longer cold and glanced down at the sleeping child on my lap. I was overcome by feelings for the girl, really a young woman, across from me, and love poured out of me, even to the child on my lap. Although I should have been very uncomfortable because of the many knees and elbows digging into me from all sides, I sat feeling wonderful. My head, full with thoughts, drove me so full of energy that my insides felt jittery and restless.

Another quick glance revealed to me that my sudden dreams were true. The girl sat innocently returning the glance. Although it was a shy glance, she comfortably held it until I looked away and focused on the green brush, which sped past the window behind her. After a sharp bump in the road, the woman next to her jumped awake suddenly. The dark-skinned girl gave her a comforting look, which could easily be interpreted as a look of true love and respect. The elderly woman smiled. As she adjusted her shawl, she glanced up at me, and seeing me look at her daughter, her smile grew greatly. She moved her eyes from me to her daughter and was herself warmed and amused by the evident feelings being sent across the crowded truck.

As time went on, I noticed that all the elderly people on the other side of the truck were looking at me. Every time I tried to sneak a look at the girl with braided hair and a green and white shawl, they all smiled and exchanged secret words. *The old lady next to her must have said something*, I thought as I tried to find a comfortable place to look. My eyes shifted from the window of the truck to someone's belt to the child on my lap and again out the window, but with each shift my eyes met the eyes of another eager and smiling person.

The light movement in my stomach remained for the remainder of the ride and grew as the truck pulled into N'Goundere and came to a bumpy halt in the middle of the dirt road. I sadly climbed out of the truck with the flow of the many people who piled out before and after me. Thrown into the dusty road, I heard numerous calls from other truck drivers and listened for the call of Garoua Boulai.

She was beautiful, I thought while staring at the *goso*, which I unconsciously fingered before putting into my mouth.

Although I was no longer facing the beautiful image that was controlling my mind, the obsession didn't fade. Instead, it grew.

After paying for the meager meal, I walked out of the wall-less, tin-roofed restaurant and into the street. I glanced over, checking to see how full my next truck was getting. A child with thin limbs and an out-of-proportion torso walked up to me with a tray that supported an aluminum teapot and two cans of Nescafé instant coffee and Nescafé evaporated milk. Although it was a hot day, I asked, "How much?"

"*Soixante-quinze*," the child said with bulging eyes and a look like he was ready to crack up laughing. Knowing that the kid was overcharging, I handed him the correct amount of 50 CFA and sat on a dirt-covered wooden bench. The child made the coffee and sat next to me waiting to have the plastic cup back.

After drinking the coffee, I walked, preoccupied, down the road and stepped up into the back of the truck heading to Garoua Boulai. Shock ran through me like a wave, starting in my head and running down to my feet. The feeling was most powerful as it passed the area just below my stomach. There she was, sitting on the thin wooden bench in the truck. The beautiful girl with the green and white shawl amazingly had transferred to the same truck as me.

Not knowing what to do, I took another step toward her and asked in French, "Is it possible for me to sit here?"

The tone of her voice said, "No, this seat is taken," but she was frantically moving the material that was bundled next to her out of the way.

She does not speak any French, I thought in despair as I sat next to her. *What am I going to do? I wonder what language she speaks: Sangho, Bantu, Bongo...?*

These and other thoughts pounded through my head. We looked at each other nervously. The natural comfort that we possessed in the other truck was gone now that the boundary and security of people between us was no longer there.

I wonder if I should try to speak to her again, I thought, but I decided that my French was too poor to use with a girl like this, and she could not understand it anyway.

We sat next to each other for what seemed like a long time, but in reality was only a matter of seconds. I had never been in a situation like this before. I was in love with a being who was in my physical grasp, but this being was unique and foreign to me. I could not express what I thought, mainly because I did not know what appropriate behavior was her custom. If I knew even what tribe she was from, I might have a chance, but no, she was a blank slate. We could see each other, but we could not intersect in any way other than the convection of emotions that told each of us separately what we were feeling and what the other was feeling. However, we could not create a unification of feeling between the two of us.

All systems failing, I had to move, so I climbed out of the truck and onto the roof flexing my arms as hard as I could as I went up, hoping she would notice. On top I found my pack and retrieved a thick novel. Once back down, beside her again I opened the book and pretended to read. Minutes went by, then she left. I continued to stare at the blurry page for a while, then put the book under the bench and left to get more coffee.

When I returned, the truck was almost full, and I quickly got into the flow of people who were squashing into the back. Unintentionally I was placed directly across from her. Our legs naturally interlocking like everyone else's, and I was embarrassed at the pale color of my legs. I had never noticed the femininity in her movements until now. I watched as she helped the lady with children next to her.

She was unaware of my stare, and her naturalness was back. The threat of us being alone was gone. The truck continued to fill up, and people started getting squashed. I reached over and picked up a young girl who belonged to a lady across from me. The child turned slowly, and when she looked at me, she went into a frightened fit of bawling. Her mother assured her that it was alright and glanced warmly at me, as did the girl next to her.

The two young children on our laps formed a wonderful bridge. The feelings of attachment and love between me and the girl with the green and white shawl were poured into the children. It was a wonderful outlet for both of us. When I saw her care for the child on her lap, I felt warm, and I knew that as I hugged and cuddled the child on my lap, she understood.

Later, as more people were picked up along the bush road, the truck became even more crowded. There was a man standing between me and the girl. Now our unspoken communication was limited to small glimpses that were permitted only when the truck braked, causing the man between us to lurch forward for a split second, long enough for a hopeful glance.

The quick looks between bumps continued but became less frequent, and I slowly fell asleep with my arms around the child. For a while every time there was a bump, I was aware of the fixed eyes across from me, and I thought that my calm sleep would appear attractive and intrigue her even more.

My dreams took me back to America where I glided smoothly over paved roads and met with friends who were colored black in my dream. When I opened my eyes, fright moved within my stomach. She was gone. The truck stopped, and she must have gotten out. I sat there feeling like I had lost something. I had closed my eyes, and she was gone. As I leaned back, I noticed a bundle of cloth. *Could it be hers?* I thought. The feeling which was becoming a normal tickle in my stomach raced yet again through me when she stepped up into the truck as it lit up with the sound of ignition. She stepped gracefully over the feet and legs of others holding her loincloth with one hand and with the other, she pulled her shawl tighter across her face as she looked over at me.

She was praying, I thought to myself, bowing her head to Allah, kissing the lucky earth. She now had a small round mark of sand on her forehead which was divided by her black tattoo. I could tell that she was in her prime years for marriage and wondered if she and her mother thought of that as they looked at me.

Would I marry her? I thought, and I fantasized about her father asking me if I would take her as a wife. I would treat her so well, with such love and respect. But no, I realized that she would become one of several wives to a man, and that she would be responsible for sitting in a hut caring for many children.

I did not realize that I was staring deep into her eyes. She noticed my sorrow and was affected by my new air of sadness. We looked at each other for a moment longer and both grew sad because of the difference between our two worlds.

Once again, the truck continued and as the day passed, more and more people got out of the truck. They simply pounded on the side of the truck, and the driver would stop, and they would walk out into the bush, usually toward their village or shanty. Although the feelings of sadness were not as strong as before, I knew that the girl would be getting off soon. The sun was past its high point in the sky, and the running of baboons across the dirt road was becoming more frequent. The heat of the sun was also tapering off, and the long shadows were starting to form behind the thick trees and elephant grass.

The lady with the three kids pounded on the truck and reached below me to retrieve a clucking chicken that was under my sandals. A thin line of fluid was left as the half dead chicken was carried away by its feet. There were now only a few people in the back of the truck. Me, three elderly men, a lady with a blue hijab, two other men, one of whom was lightheartedly trying to seduce a woman half his age, and the beautiful girl and her mother.

When the truck came to another stop, one of the men, who was fumbling around the floor looking for his machete, pulled out a book which was very torn, stepped on, and was missing its cover. He pounded the dirt off it with his hand and said something in a native tongue. Before I could react, the girl across from me pointed excitedly toward me and replied in what seemed to be the same language. The guy chuckled and handed the thrashed book to me.

I felt wonderful. I could tell that she reacted more excitedly about helping me than she would have if the book were to belong to anyone else. I felt that she made a great effort to show that she cared, even for a book of mine, and wanted it to be returned to me promptly and correctly and with care. I simply felt that she cared for me.

I replied, "*Merci*," hoping that she understood.

The time came. The truck slowly rolled to a stop, and she started to get up. I felt as if I were going to explode. I wanted so badly to say something, but what, and in what language?

Wait, I said to myself, *Stop*. My stomach was moving so fast that I felt that it was growing in size. It tingled so much that it felt almost numb. *Say something*, I said to myself, my heart racing. *Get out. You have communicated without a common language before.* I did not know what to do, and I felt surges of hot and cold panic fly through my body as I tried to figure out what to do.

As the truck pulled away, I looked back hoping to get one more glimpse of her, or even of her green and white shawl, but the small scene behind the glassless window filled with rising dust as the knobby tires of the truck sped over the dry road.

Your Turn to Explore

Have you ever wanted to connect with somebody but were held back by fear or something else? Who or where was it, and what happened?

Are there missed opportunities in life, or do things happen exactly as they are supposed to happen? Can you think of a missed opportunity in your life? If so, what is one thing good that came from the situation?

Do Something Extraordinary: While in Africa, I wasn't brave enough to follow my desire to really connect with the girl in the truck, but I did connect with her through warmth in my actions and a smile. Today or tomorrow, connect with at least five people you don't know by smiling broadly, making eye contact, and if appropriate, just say hi.

FOUR

SECRET RITUAL

Washington State, USA. 1973 and 1979. Four and Ten Years Old

I told Elaine that I wanted to take the training wheels off my bicycle. She thought it was an admirable idea.

We walked over to my house. After turning my little orange and yellow bike upside down, I dug through my dad's tools until I found what I thought would work. After a lot of fumbling around with different tools and a lot of encouragement from Elaine, I somehow got the training wheels off.

We pushed the bike through the grass up to the tiny private road that ran between my house and her grandparents'. With Elaine standing on the white cement of her grandparents' driveway, I positioned the bike, aiming down the middle of the blacktop, as if I were a test pilot for a manned military rocket ship.

"I'll give you a kiss if you make it," Elaine said, smiling shyly.

Now that was motivation.

I backed up the bike, so the right pedal was at the top of its radius. I pushed off and pedaled with all my might. I probably made about four rotations on the pedals as the bike arched a wide path to the right. I crashed mostly onto the grass at the side of the road.

Does that count? I wondered.

It did. Elaine walked over as if I were the winner of a grand prix car race, said, "Good job," and kissed me right on my cheek. My first kiss. I was four years old, and it was wonderful.

***

It was the second grade. Julie Fenna and I found ourselves under Mrs. Onneta's desk. It was our little fort during class reading time.

Julie told me, "You can kiss me on the cheek." I looked out from under the desk and saw the bottom half of Mrs. Onneta's legs near the chalkboard, and then I quickly pecked Julie on the side of her face.

Julie and I walked home together. When we reached the small wooded area between our houses, I'd get to give her another peck on the cheek.

After a few days of this, as I was going in for my daily peck on her cheek, Julie informed me, "You can kiss me on the lips."

Wow, that is special.

I gave her a tight pursed-lipped kiss on her little red lips with my eyes closed. I loved it.

We went separate ways. I ran up the steep shortcut on Golden Given Hill through the trees. As soon as I got home, I ran into the kitchen and told my mom that I had kissed Julie. My mom asked, "Why did you do that?"

"Julie asked me to," I answered, now questioning if it had been a good idea to tell her.

Once my mom's initial angry reaction had passed, she more calmly said, "Well, you shouldn't. You might get a disease."

Even in second grade, I thought that was a dumb response, but I guess my mom was simply trying to figure out a way to make me keep my lips to myself.

Julie and I never kissed again. Although we were still good friends, we eventually quit walking home together.

***

Second grade wasn't my finest academic year. Although I didn't officially flunk, my teacher and the principal told my parents that it might be a good idea if I were to repeat the year. It was up to us, though, and trying to be progressive, my parents said that ultimately it would be my decision. My mom did help by suggesting that we make a pros and cons list to decide what would be the best. We spent two days returning to the list, adding pros and cons when we thought of them. In the end, the list was tied at eight points to eight. On the day the decision had to be made, my mom said, "Okay, just think of one more pro or con."

"Betty Iverson," I said as the beautiful image of the little blonde girl who lived down the street popped into my head. Betty was in the first grade, going into second, so I rarely saw her because of our different grade levels. I loved the idea of getting to spend more time with her.

Betty Iverson, I wrote boldly at the bottom of the pros side of the list for repeating the second grade.

"Okay," my mom said smiling. "It is settled then."

I think my mom secretly wanted me to stay back, so she was happy with anything on the pros side, even little Betty Iverson.

A few weeks into second grade, I had gotten to know Betty better. I didn't even have to write her a *"Will you go with me? Check the box: yes, no, or maybe"* letter. We were playing in the huge barn on the ranch she lived on. We were sitting and hiding in a two-wheeled horse buggy that was propped up against the wall.

"Do you want to make out or kiss?" Betty asked with the air of someone with a lot of experience, but really neither of us even knew what "make out" meant.

Even still I answered, "Make out."

"How about we just kiss?" responded Betty.

"Okay," I agreed, happy to be in the barn with Betty. We pecked each other on the lips, giggled, and ran out of the barn to play outside.

I mention these little anecdotes of innocent childhood "romance" because I really enjoyed the high and low emotions as we blameless kids had fun experimenting with relationships. I chased Erin Walten all through grade school, and I even "got married" with Amy Evans.

***

Not everything that happened in the woods between my house and Julie Fenna's was innocent.

Our neighborhood, near the top of Golden Given Hill, was wonderful. There were many houses with kids, and we had a lot of space to play tag, kick-the-can, football, and baseball. Near my house, there was one set of duplexes, and beyond that was a nice wide-open trailer park with six mobile homes permanently set in a nice row in the middle of a giant, well-kept lawn.

The duplex had a pretty frequent turnover of residents, and when I was in the third grade, there was a family from Germany living in one of them. One of the kids, named Erwin, was about a year older than me, and we'd play together sometimes. Erwin was a bit strange, but maybe it was just his accent, and we generally got along well. Erwin had an older brother named Tom. I really didn't know Tom that well because he was much older than us, probably by about eight or nine years.

One day, Tom saw me just at the top of Golden Given Hill, right in front of my house. I was on my way home from school.

"Hi, Erik," Tom said.

"Hi, Tom."

"Hey, Erik, do you want to see something?"

"Sure," I said, "What is it?"

"I'll show you, come on," Tom said as he began walking down the small path back into the woods.

Immediately I followed, curious about what he was going to show me.

When we got about halfway into the woods, Tom suggested we get off the small trail a bit and go over behind a group of trees that I'd played in and climbed many times.

"Look," Tom said, pulling a *Playboy* magazine from his thin jacket.

"Wow," I said, trying to be cool.

Prior to this, I'd seen one centerfold in my life. It was a relatively modest reclining woman with dark brown hair, a full figure, and no clothes. I'm not sure where my friend Bart had gotten it, but I'd seen it and thought it made me more grown-up that I had seen it.

Now, as Tom started slowly flipping through a few pages, he suggested, "Let's sit here."

We sat next to each other on the grass between the trees. I sat for a moment looking at a few of the pictures, but it didn't feel good. I didn't like it, but I didn't want Tom to know this.

"I'm going to go," I said to Tom. I began to stand up.

"No, wait," Tom told me. Tom's lips looked dry, and he licked them. "You're not going to tell anyone about this, are you?"

"No, I won't."

"You promise, right?" Tom asked, "It is our secret, right?"

"Yeah," I said, wondering why an 18 or 19-year-old would be so concerned.

"Good," Tom replied, "but just to make sure, there is a ritual that people do to make sure a secret is not broken."

"Really," I responded, thinking that a ritual sounded fun.

"Yeah, you want to do it?"

"Okay."

"Sit back down," Tom said, "And, with this ritual, a promise can't be broken. It is like making a pact, and a secret will be safe."

After I sat down, Tom said that the first thing he had to do was to put a blindfold on me. At ten years old, I didn't think it was strange that Tom already had a blindfold in his pocket. It was a black length of material about three inches wide and about a yard long. I helped him by leaning in as he reached out to tie the blindfold over my eyes and around my head.

Once the blindfold was in place, nothing happened for a few seconds. Then I felt Tom unbuttoning my pants.

"What are you doing?" I exclaimed.

"Oh, this is part of the ritual. I learned how to do it in a magazine," he explained, "and you are going to like it."

After he unbuttoned my pants, he pulled them all the way down to my ankles.

I heard Tom breathing heavily.

"What are you doing?" I asked, pulling the blindfold up to see what was happening.

"Don't!" Tom shouted angrily. "The ritual doesn't work without the blindfold!"

Tom tried to push the blindfold back over my face, but I had already seen that Tom was unbuttoning his own pants.

Horrified, I sprung from my sitting position, pulled up my pants, and ran as fast as I could.

"Wait!" Tom yelled. He caught up with me near the top of the hill and along the side of the road.

"You won't tell anyone, will you?" he asked me.

With my pants up and the blindfold off, I immediately felt better. "No," I said. I agreed that I wouldn't tell a soul.

Tom and I casually walked back up to the top of Golden Given Hill together.

"Bye, Tom," I said and walked to my house.

I don't feel mentally scarred from the incident with Tom. I feel angry that I let it go as far as it did, and I feel horror at what could have happened. I feel angry that I didn't say anything, but fortunately the episode wasn't worse. After this occurred, I quickly forgot about it and started looking for the next little girl whom I could ask to go steady with. But the fact is, what Tom did was a crime, and I should have told someone.

Your Turn to Explore

Have you ever had something happen to you that no one knows about? If so, is the time right to tell someone you trust?

How is sharing (under the right circumstances) a way for people to find healing from terrible incidents?

Do Something Extraordinary: I feel wonderful thinking about my little childhood crushes. I wouldn't call them romantic love, but even those youthful moments are wonderful feelings of love and joy to have shared with others. Sadly, there exists those whose intentions are less than innocent, and I think it is sad how often these individuals get away with what they do because people (like my younger self) don't tell. If you have something in your past that you desire to share but don't know how to do it, think of the one person with whom you'd trust enough to share, and just tell them about it.

FIVE

IT MATTERED

Alaska, USA. 1993. Twenty-Four Years Old

We made it until about 2 pm before neither of us could handle it any longer. It was an unexciting job, and neither John nor I could get into it that day. We were painting a house, and on that particular day, it was a struggle from the start. We finally decided that we had to get out, so we packed up and took off.

We didn't know exactly where we were going to go, but we had to get outside into the great Alaskan fresh air. I grabbed my black cowboy hat and changed into a brown wool flannel and my cowboy boots. John just grabbed a baseball cap and put a vest on over his work clothes. Our first stop was the liquor store.

"ID please," the woman behind the counter said.

"Are you kidding?" I responded. "Come on. I've come into this store once a week for over a month, and you still don't recognize me?"

"Sorry. It's been a long day, and I didn't recognize the hat. And, you're usually a dirty mess when you come in here," she said smiling now that she recognized me.

This part was true, because I'd often come by dirty from head to toe on my way home from working construction in the mud all day.

Without checking my ID, she punched the price of the Jack Daniel's into her register and said, "Fourteen thirty-two." Then she said, "Make it 14 bucks, and if you tell it to me, I won't forget your name next time you come in."

"Erik," I said as I smiled at her. She pushed her long, dark hair over her shoulder and held the bottle out to me.

"See you next time, Erik."

"Certainly," I said as John and I walked out.

Our next stop was the gun store. I already had my nickel-plated 7.5-inch barrel .44 Magnum Ruger Blackhawk with me. Indeed, I loved this revolver. "Old Faithful" was a single-action beauty with wooden grips, and she was always with me in Alaska. John had a 9mm Semi-Automatic Springfield. We bought a few boxes of ammo, jumped into John's large truck, and headed out of Eagle River to the north.

We were quick to open the Jack, which helped ease our guilt for leaving work early, and by the time we got off the paved Glenn Highway, we were already a bit buzzed. We were heading into the area of Knik to the southwest of Wasilla, which is outside of the Anchorage Basin and where some real Alaska wild begins.

When we'd go out to this area for construction jobs, we'd always carry guns for two reasons. First, for the rare chance an agitated grizzly would turn up. Second, because of the hermits and other untamed and potentially unhinged folk who lived out in this remote area for reasons they might not want to share.

We'd been driving on dirt roads for quite a while when we decided to get out of the truck. We pulled off to the side near a creek. It was probably about five o'clock at this point, and we hadn't considered food—until now.

"I have some fishing rods in the back of the truck," John said.

So we caught a few large trout, built a fire, and ate them right there on the rocky shoreline. While normally we'd cook freshly caught fish with salt, pepper, and lemon, it was delicious with nothing at all.

As we walked back to the truck, we saw a shortcut, which was about a 15-foot climb up a steep cliff. I made it up easily, but when John tried to do the same with his tackle box in one hand, right before reaching the top he ended up sliding down the 15 feet of sharp rocks. His jeans were massively ripped, and blood was gushing out down the front of his legs. His knees got pretty chewed up.

"Oh, shit," John hollered while sliding backward down to the bank. Upon landing on the boulders at the bottom, he announced, "I'm okay." Next, he limped around the longer way. He figured he wouldn't feel the pain until the next morning.

Near the truck we decided to fire off a few rounds before moving on, so we found a nice bank, threw a few beer cans in front of it, and started murdering Budweisers. John's 9mm emitted a sharp *bang, bang, bang,* and a thunderous *BOOM* came from my .44.

As we started to drive away, we noticed the odd sign announcing: "SHOOTING PROHIBITED! Violators May Be Prosecuted." It was a difficult sign to read due to the many bullet holes shot through it. That and the blue spray paint over it reading: "Abolish All Prosecutors."

Our Jack Daniel's was almost out, so John and I decided to find Blacky's, a remote watering hole kind of in the middle of nowhere. When we got there, a band was setting up in the yard, so we bought a few beers and sat on the front porch steps. It was getting dark now, and there were more people at Blacky's than I'd ever seen.

Blacky's had a large gravel parking lot, and as we sat there, a guy kept taking people over to his motorcycle, starting it up, then turning it off, and returning. He did this about four times, when I turned to John, asking, "What the heck? If he wants to ride, ride. Why in the world does he keep showing people his bike and coming back?"

John said, "Don't tell me, tell him."

John and I were both pretty lit up by this point. When the guy returned and passed the porch, I did tell him.

"I'm trying to, man," the guy said. "I can't get it into first gear."

"Oh," I said. "Can I try?"

"Sure," he responded.

As I walked over to the bike, I saw it was a small 500cc Honda. I threw my leg over the bike, pulled in the clutch, started it, and tried to press down on the shifter to find first. It did not work. I tried again. Nothing. Then, I up-shifted to second, third, fourth, fifth, and then backward, and the bike slipped into first gear smoothly.

In my excitement, I dropped the clutch and twisted on the throttle. The rear tire of the bike spun wildly, and I leaned the bike over, spinning it around, and started a donut.

Later, John told me that when the taillight came around in the dark and with all the dust flying, he thought I dropped the bike. Then the taillight came around again, and he thought the same thing.

In my drunken excitement, I just kept doing circular donuts kicking up gravel and dirt in every direction, and then finally the bike slid out from under me and went spinning on its side in the parking lot, and I ended up on my back looking up at the crowd that had gathered to watch.

As soon as I crashed, the owner of the bike came running toward me. I thought he'd be pissed, but as I was putting my hands up to defend myself from a punch, the guy grabbed my hand, saying, "Thanks, man. No one else was able to get it going. Awesome job."

I couldn't believe it. He was obviously much higher and happier that I was. We walked over and picked up the bike together. He rode the bike in a big circle in the parking lot and then proudly parked it in the grass over by the band.

Cracking up about this, John and I decided to move on. We were driving wildly down dirt roads in the dim light. We were now miles away from any semblance of civilization, sliding around corners and going fast over rising hills and bumps. Then we got the guns out. I was shooting out the passenger side, and John was shooting with his left hand out of the driver's side window. Anything was fair game: trees, stumps, squirrels, but any squirrels hit were truly incidental because we couldn't hit the broad side of a barn if we wanted to at this point.

"Oh, shit," John announced.

"What?"

"We're almost out of gas."

I asked, "Any idea how far we are from a road?"

"None at all," John responded.

In our sudden anxiety, John turned down the loud radio and rolled up his window as if that would help save gas.

We slowed to a normal pace and then stopped the truck to think.

John said, "I'm sure we won't make it back the way we came on the amount of gas left." So the only option was to push forward and hope for the best.

We drove relatively slowly, for a bit, and then we saw a house. It seemed we were in luck. But it wasn't just a house, it also had two 10- by 40-foot mobile homes that had been welded together to make a small lounge. After parking the truck, we saw a beautiful, large dog limping towards us as we walked up to the entrance. We patted the friendly dog on the head and stepped in.

The "lounge" was mostly just a rectangular bar with an open middle and bottles in the center. It was like what you'd find at most airport bars, only this was way different since we were in the woods, in a homemade mobile home with fake wood paneling walls for décor. There were two other men sitting at the bar. One was on a corner near the door, and the other was at the far end of the bar on the same side.

John and I walked up to the bar, and there was a beautiful woman pouring a drink for one of the men. Her long, black hair and wide face showed that she was Inuit Eskimo.

She approached us and said, "Hi, what can I get you?"

I have no idea where my next move came from. I was already a bit buzzed, but for some reason, I wanted to try something different. "Green Label Jack Daniel's," I said.

The woman started cracking up, looked at John, and said, "He isn't from around here, is he?"

John laughed, looking at me, and asked, "What were you thinking?"

To the barmaid, he said, "Two Jack and Cokes."

"Now, that's better," she replied with a giant smile as she turned and fixed the drinks.

After a few sips of the strong Jack and Coke, John asked the barmaid, who we learned was named Rochelle, "Is there anywhere to get gas around here?"

Rochelle laughed almost as hard as she had when I'd ordered the fancy drink.

"Not for a while, honey," she answered. "The closest is a 7-Eleven, but it is back on the highway about 40 miles from here."

"Oh, shit," John said again. Turning to me, he said, "We're screwed."

"Our truck is on empty," I explained to Rochelle.

"Oh no. Well, you can't stay here," she continued joking.

"I can help," said the old guy at the end of the bar.

"Really," I said, looking at him hopefully.

"Yeah, I live just next door, and I've got a bit of gas for my lawnmower."

"Awesome," John said enthusiastically. "That's very cool of you."

We told Rochelle that we'd be back, and we walked out with the old-timer. When we got to his toolshed, his gas can was empty.

A bit distraught at first, we three drunken men all seemed to have the same idea at the same time. "Let's just use the gas *in* the lawnmower," the guy announced as we all looked at the red push-mower in the center of the shed.

I'm not sure how we actually did it, but I do know that a long, stiff wire was involved to open the stopper at the bottom of the truck's fuel tank opening. I know we had a funnel. Totally inebriated, the three of us, trying to manage the stopper, the funnel, and an awkward 50-pound lawn mower, hoisted the entire lawn mower upside down along the side of the truck.

The entire time we were monkeying with the lawn mower, the gentle dog limped around with us as if trying to help, wagging his tail in encouragement.

I'm sure there were a thousand easier ways to accomplish the task, but we didn't think of them, and somehow, we got some gas into the truck.

Back in the bar, we celebrated our success. The guy who had given us the gas refused to take any money, but we did buy him a drink.

After a few more drinks we all became very familiar with everyone. John finally asked, "What happened to the dog?"

Rochelle said, "Someone shot him with a shotgun."

"What!" John and I said in unison.

"Yeah, it was a few weeks ago."

"Who did it?" John asked.

"Some asshole up the road."

John and I felt protective of the gentle dog, and I think we also wanted to impress Rochelle. We were drunk and pissed, and we asked Rochelle to tell us where the guy lived because we wanted to shoot up his house. Rochelle was thrilled that we wanted to get revenge for her, but thank God, she didn't tell us.

Before John and I left, we hugged everyone in the bar. Before taking off, we decided that we wanted to show Rochelle that we were serious about what we had said. So we got into the truck, turned on the ignition, and as John hit the accelerator spinning the rear tires, I fired off two large booms from the .44, and John ripped off ten quick shots from the 9mm.

As we did this, we noticed a guy in the parking lot walking toward the door. Once he heard the shots, he ran and almost dove through the entrance. Rochelle would certainly know that we were serious about shooting up the guy's house for her.

As we rolled down the dirt road, John was again driving quickly, and the music was loud. The windows were open and *Ramblin' Man* by The Allman Brothers was cranking out of the radio. We sped along in the cold, feeling great. When we finally reached a paved road, we headed south until seeing the 7-Eleven.

John started pumping the gas, and I walked into the store, waltzed over to the freezers, and picked up a 12-pack of beer.

"No-can-do," the tall and skinny guy at the register said. "Beer and wine sales end at midnight."

"Come on," I said, reeking of gas, booze, and gunpowder, "just one 12-pack."

"Uhh," the guy stuttered, "Um, okay. Just one."

When I looked down to get my wallet, I realized why the guy had suddenly become so polite. I forgot that my giant revolver was still sticking out of the front beltline of my pants. If it had been in a holster, the guy wouldn't have cared a bit, but seeing the handle of the gun sticking out of the front of my pants bank-robber-style would have seemed quite peculiar. This wasn't my intention, but it did help us get more beer.

On the long drive back to Eagle River, John and I spoke about family, friends, relationships, jobs, and everything else going on in our lives. And how it could be better.

We were step-brothers. His dad and my mom had gotten married about a year earlier, and it was the first time we went really deep with each other on everything from secret wishes for the future to regrets from the past. It was an amazing time of trying to figure everything out and make resolutions on how to improve ourselves. I think both of us were shaken from the recent divorce of my parents and the death of his mom, and we were both struggling to find out exactly what we wanted out of life. The day we had just lived was a result of that search, and I think we both wondered if reckless partying was really the direction we wanted our lives to continue in.

As we neared Eagle River, our conversation wasn't quite finished, so John pulled off the side of the road. We cracked open one last Budweiser and finished the start of our discussion about life. It was wonderful, and we appreciated the time together. It was about three in the morning after our wild and reckless binge, and work was supposed to begin in four hours.

We agreed to be responsible. We made a pact to show up on time, and we did. And it mattered.

Your Turn to Explore

Have you ever been shaken up by a difficult situation in life that made you wonder how you could proceed with, much less enjoy, your life afterward? When was it, and did you make any changes or are you still struggling?

What are the most common events that cause pain in people's lives? What is the best way to find comfort?

Do Something Extraordinary: John and I both experienced loss through the divorce of my parents and the death of his mother, but when we finally came together and loved each other as family, we were able to see some good from two bad situations. Think of a time when something beyond your control made you terribly sad and think of at least one good thing that happened because of the difficult situation you went through.

SIX

CHASING THE GIRL ON THE BUS

Virginia, USA. 1994. Twenty-Five Years Old

I had just started graduate school at the University of Virginia. It was about two weeks into the school year. Returning from classes, I was sitting in a campus bus heading to my apartment. The day was average until an extremely cute girl stepped up the large steps and into the aisle of the bus. I was captured by her from the moment I saw her. My heart leapt when, although there were other empty seats, she asked if anyone was sitting next to me.

"No," I excitedly responded, hoping she wouldn't notice how happy I was that she might sit next to me.

"Thanks," she calmly responded and casually scooted into the seat.

Trying not to seem nervous, I was desperately trying to think of something to say to her. The bus lurched ahead, and I knew I didn't have much time. Since it was a pleasant and sunny Friday afternoon, I had an idea.

"Do you know any good places to hike around here?" I asked.

"Um," she started to say.

"I just got here, and it is a wonderful day, but I don't know the area yet," I continued not even giving her time to think. I was begging for the opportunity for her to give me advice about Charlottesville and maybe even be willing to show me around.

"Well, we are close to the Blue Ridge Mountains, you know," she said. I had an idea but really didn't know much at all.

"Not really. I haven't had a chance to explore yet," I said.

"Wait," she said excitedly, "I know of a great spot. It is called Humpback Rock."

Laughing hysterically to myself that she suggested something with the name "hump" in it, I tried to hide my immaturity and remain cool.

I responded that I didn't know where that was.

My heart was beating more quickly than normal. I was totally infatuated with the lovely girl who was sitting next to me. She had kind of bobbed jet-black hair, alabaster skin, very bright eyes, and a charming smile. She gave me a general idea where it was, and the conversation turned to our professors. Apparently, she was in an anthropology class with one of my advisors. I also learned that she was born in Vietnam, and her name was Zip.

When I got back to my place, I called another student in my department named Rich, and we drove up and hiked Humpback Rock.

After the hike, as soon as I got back to my apartment, I could think of nothing but the girl I had met on the bus. I had to find her again.

I dug out the UVA student directory, and starting with A, I scanned every single one of the 19 thousand names in the campus phonebook, looking for any Vietnamese last name. Each time I found one, I eagerly checked if the first name was Zip. From A to Z, I did not succeed.

Weeks went by, but I never saw the beautiful girl from the bus. It was as if she were a phantom.

However, there was one other girl that I occasionally saw in the student cafeteria whom I also found very attractive. She also had black hair and beautiful skin. She was quite skinny and often wore a long purple jacket that made her look like a young, but unpretentious, fashion model.

Eight months passed, and I still never saw the charming girl from the bus, but one day, when I was sitting at a campus café with Rich, the girl from the cafeteria walked up and started speaking with Rich. I was stupefied and just sat there trying not to be obvious in my admiration of her. The girl and Rich worked in catering together and spoke for a few minutes about work.

She said, "Okay, see you, Rich."

Rich said, "Bye, Zip."

What!!!! I said to myself. *It's her! It's Zip, the same girl from the bus.*

Apparently, I hadn't found her name in the phonebook because although pronounced "zip," I would learn that her name is actually spelled D-i-e-p. I don't know how I didn't make the connection earlier. My heart raced wildly.

"Rich," I said excitedly, "do you remember me telling you about the girl on the bus before we went hiking at the start of the school year?"

"Of course," Rich answered, "you didn't talk about anything else on the hike."

"Well," I said, "that is her!"

That evening, I was sitting at the cafeteria with one of my suitemates, Ton, and I was anxiously looking around the entire time. Then I finally saw her. She was sitting at the end of one of the long tables across from a friend. I gathered my courage, Ton wished me luck, and I walked over to the table.

I tried to act like I was just passing by and happened to notice her. Then I knelt down and said, "Hi, do you ever remember having a conversation with me on the bus? It was about eight months ago, and we spoke about hiking and Dr. Reese."

She looked at me a bit surprised and then replied, "Yes, I remember."

There was a joyful look in her eye, which made me very happy.

"Great to see you again," I said as casually as I could, and I stood up and walked away, knowing that first contact had been made.

It wasn't long after this encounter that Diep would regularly walk through the library with not only her books but a motorcycle helmet too. We'd started studying together. We would ride, study, and take long walks around the UVA grounds.

On one notable night at about one in the morning, we woke everyone up by pressing the Edgar Allen Poe information button outside of his old room from when he was a student at the university. At first, we thought it was funny how loud the recording was, but as the long monologue continued, we felt we had an obligation to stay through the whole thing. In the end, we were horribly embarrassed as students in nearby rooms facing the lawn opened their doors and peeked out at us as we tried to inconspicuously slip away. It was simply an amazing time of getting to know each other and loving the company. I felt warm every time Diep and I were within 100 feet of each other.

Then I graduated.

After going to Los Angeles for a while, I left for Thailand. I planned on spending two years there, teaching English and training Muay Thai boxing. Diep called me every week, even from thousands of miles away. After about seven months, I really began to wish I were near her again, so one night on the phone I asked, "Diep, what would you think if I moved back to Virginia? No strings attached if things don't work out, but would you want me to do this?"

There might have been a brief pause, but she said that she would like that.

I flew to Seattle, bought a motorcycle, rode to L.A. to take care of a few things, and headed east. Since I hadn't seen Diep in over a year, I wanted to get there as quickly as possible. I made it on my old 1977 Harley-Davidson Ironhead in 3.5 days, including 16 hours of breakdown time in El Paso. I spent about 20 hours per day in the saddle of the old bike with only a few hours of rest here and there on the side of the road. I had one thing on my mind the whole time, and it was Diep. I couldn't wait to be with her again, and I was not disappointed seeing her when I arrived. I was again able to spend beautiful days and delightful evenings with the angel who'd sat next to me on the bus.

Your Turn to Explore

Have you ever been dumbstruck with "love at first sight"? Who was it, and did anything become of it?

What makes someone immediately attracted to another person?

Do Something Extraordinary: While sitting next to the strikingly attractive girl on the bus, it would have been easy for me to submit to my nervousness and do nothing, and I'm very glad this isn't what happened. If you are single, next time you see someone who absolutely strikes you with "awe," don't let the moment pass. Find something to say to them. If you are in a relationship, tell your partner how you felt the first time you saw them.

SEVEN

REFLECTIONS ON LOVE

I'm going to go right out and say it—I think love is the best thing in life.

Love encompasses a multitude of things, ranging from friendship, familial affection, and romantic love, to a love of God. I think love can be one and all these things, and I also think that love is one of the best ways we can see meaning in our lives. Love takes us beyond ourselves. When we love, the warm feelings we get are usually a byproduct of wanting another to feel wonderful by loving or helping the other person.

In the narratives in the preceding section, when I think of Alaywe in the Amazon, the girl with the green and white shawl in Africa, my connection with John in Alaska, all of the little crushes I had when I was younger, and finally Diep, the stunning girl on the bus, I wish all these beloved people in my life to feel joy, happiness, and success in their lives because even though I'll never see most of them again, I love them, and I desire that they are well.

Love is a focus in this book because love is an extension of the four pillars of meaning on which I structured my first book,

Ordinary to Extraordinary. However, the four pillars of meaning—belonging, purpose, transcendence, and storytelling—don't quite complete the whole story of meaning. As Emily Esfahani Smith writes near the end of *The Power of Meaning*, "Love ... is at the center of the meaningful life. Love cuts through each of the pillars of meaning ... The act of love begins with the very definition of meaning: it begins by stepping outside of the self to connect with and contribute to something bigger."

Love is present everywhere, both within the comfortable center of ordinary, along the widening circles of exploration, and all the way to the far reaches of the edge. Love isn't bound by space or time. Do you love anyone who lives in a different city or country? Do you love anyone who has died, or can you imagine loving someone not yet born?

Also, love manifests itself very differently, depending on its location on the spectrum from the comfortable center to the sizzling edge. The very reassuring marital love as expressed by Soren Kierkegaard has a depth and stability to it that can bind two individuals with an unbreakable, calm force, yet love can also be the sometimes erratic infatuation we get when we desire to be closer to someone who may or may not love us back. These passionate feelings stir something in us as we walk the edge of uncertainty, hope, and desire. Do you remember your first crush, first heartbreak, or first kiss? Sometimes in our lives, it is in this vulnerable space along the edge where we feel most excited, alive, and driven to be better than we were yesterday in an attempt to add love to our tomorrow.

With this idea in mind, love, by definition, pulls us out of the self-absorbed, ego-centric space where it is so easy for many of us to find ourselves. Love allows us to recognize our value reflected in others, those whom we love. When the Beatles released their poignant song, *All You Need Is Love*, they understood both how simple and how all-encompassing that very short phrase is in describing everything essential to being human.

Your Turn to Explore

Who do you love? What do you love? Why? Explore your thoughts about love and reflect on all the areas in your life where love is present. Is your life full with love, or is there something you could do to inject more love into your life? As you're thinking about love, also think of all the individuals who love you. Ask yourself if they also feel love from you. There are many things in life I think we can skimp on, but in my opinion, love isn't one of them. Love now, love always.

Do Something Extraordinary: Tell your partner or spouse that you love them. Tell your children that you love them. Now, think of someone whom you love, but to whom you've never verbally expressed this. It could be a parent, a friend, anyone. Today or tomorrow, tell them that you love them.

PS: If you don't feel love in your life, tell someone, and I bet they'll tell you that you're wrong.

BONUS CHALLENGE

Sometimes love is so close in our lives, we take it for granted, but don't let the comfort of love with your partner or spouse become boring love. Think of ten ways you can communicate love to your partner like buying flowers for no reason, suggesting a candle-lit dinner for no reason, writing a short love note and placing it in the book they are reading. Choose four things and add them to your calendar so that you do one per week this month. I am smiling now as I write this, knowing how much you and your lover will enjoy these tiny gestures of affection.

YOUR FREE GIFT

Believe it or not, keeping up a steady flow of gestures express-ing love, respect, and affection is not as simple as it sounds. With our busy lives of work, children, and activities, it is easy to neglect probably the most important person in your life. Don't let this happen. I've created a free interactive calen-dar filled with suggestions on what you can do to make your partner feel loved every week. The suggestions are almost exclusively no cost or very low-cost ideas, and there are two formats based on whether your partner is male or female. To get this wonderful relationship tool, simply email me with AFFECTION CALENDAR [MALE or FEMALE] in the subject line. Email Erik@ErikSeversen.com or go to www.ErikSeversen. com.

PART 2

GROWTH

The real contest ... is striving to reach your personal best, and that is totally under your control.

—John Wooden

EIGHT

JAPANESE

Kanuma, Japan. 1990. Twenty Years Old

I can speak Japanese, I thought to myself. After all, I had my own wheels, a *gomi* bicycle (which I shamelessly pulled from the curb in front of a house on garbage day), I had a job, an apartment, and I had been in Japan for about a month.

Yeah, I can do it, I thought again when I decided that I wanted to go out to dinner all by myself.

I was living in the rural town of Kanuma, located in the beautiful mountains between Nikko and Utsunomiya, about an hour's bullet train ride north of Tokyo. Green River College had hired me to work at a brand-new branch campus in Japan, and I was eager to learn as much as I could while there. English was very rarely spoken by the inhabitants in Kanuma, and I decided that even if I found someone who could speak English, I wouldn't use a word of it the entire evening.

It really wasn't a big deal, but I was excited when I pulled my squeaking, beat-up ten-speed from the tiny carport of my apartment, threw my leg over the seat, and pedaled into the street, turning right past the lush green rice patties that flanked the road. After less than a mile, I was entering the center of Kanuma. I had a restaurant picked out. It was one I'd never been to before, but I heard it was very traditional as well as very good.

After placing my bicycle next to a few others that leaned against the side of the building, I walked in. I bowed slightly as I passed under the flags with faded Japanese characters hanging above the entrance.

As my eyes adjusted to the dark room, a bright-eyed young woman in a green and gold kimono approached me. In a cheerful high voice, she said, "*Irasshaimass.*"

"*Kon ban wa,*" I responded, proud that I was on the right track. What did I say to her? I said, "Good evening."

She then said a string of words. I could tell that she was asking if I wanted to sit, and I confidently replied, "*Hai,*" confirming that, yes, that was exactly what I wanted.

The restaurant was a bit larger than most of the small places in Kanuma. It was made of a beautiful dark wood. It was only partially full. As I was seated by myself at a table for four, I said, "*Arigato.*"

The waitress rushed away with short quick steps in her bamboo sandals and returned with a thick menu. With a polite dip of her head, she spoke again. I could tell she was asking what I wanted to drink.

I glanced at the menu but didn't have to look at it to say, "*Asahi biru, onegaishimasu,*" or "I would like Asahi beer, please." Being the legal limit of 20 years old, I felt mature ordering the beer, and I thought that my knowing which type of Japanese beer I wanted without looking made me seem even more fluent in Japanese.

I was really starting to feel proud of myself, but once the waitress left to get the drink, I noticed that the writing in the menu was entirely in Kanji and Hiragana. I could understand neither alphabet. It included no Romaji or Katakana, the two alphabets I could sometimes figure out. I wasn't going to break my rule though. I could tell how impressed the waitress was with my Japanese, and I certainly wasn't going to ruin that.

Having absolutely no idea what anything written on the menu was, I simply selected a page that most likely listed main course meals. I was scanning this page when the waitress returned and poured half of the bottle of beer into my thin glass. Next, she carefully placed the bottle on the wooden lacquered table and spoke.

I didn't understand a word of what she said, but I could tell she was asking what I wanted to order. Again, not breaking my rule of speaking any English, I pointed at something in the middle of the menu and held it up for her to see. I had pulled it off. She said, "Thank you," in Japanese and again hurried away.

I sat alone sipping my beer, looking around the dim room, and occasionally smiling toward people at tables with whom I made eye contact. I began thinking of the friends I had made at the school where I was working and about the decrepit Bonsai tree I recently purchased from the missing-two-fingers Yakuza mafia runner who was essentially selling Bonsais door-to-door to collect "neighborhood watch" money.

It didn't take long, though, before the waitress returned. Smiling as always, she politely put a very large plate in front of me. I smiled, but my heart sank when I looked down at the plate. It certainly wasn't what I was in the mood for. The plate contained long thin strips of raw meat. It was a large plate full of the bright red beef strips with one single raw egg in the middle.

"Ugghh," I quietly uttered to myself after she left.

I stared at the plate for a moment, but I wasn't going to be a fool and let her know that I had mistakenly ordered the wrong thing. Although it crossed my mind, I didn't even consider trying to exchange it for something else. I took another sip of my Asahi, picked up my chopsticks, and went to work on the meat. Since I was alone, and I was in no mood to savor the raw meat, it didn't take long for me to finish. As I put the last piece of the red meat in my mouth, I was actually happy that I had finished. That's when the gentle waitress walked up to my table with a little grill.

Oh no, I said to myself. I was supposed to cook the meat at the table.

Still holding the small grill, the waitress in the green and gold kimono didn't know what to do. Our eyes met, and her pale face had a look of horrified, embarrassed shock. It wasn't clear if she was embarrassed for herself or for me. I could tell she didn't know what to do with the grill. Finally, after a still moment, she quickly put the grill on the table next to my empty plate and walked away even faster than she had before. If I didn't want to look like a fool for not speaking Japanese, I certainly succeeded in making myself look like an idiot by scarfing down the raw meat and egg before cooking it.

I don't care, I thought. *I'm still not going to speak any English. In fact, I'm going to make her think I wanted to eat the meat raw.* I knew in my mind that this was ridiculous, but when the waitress, still looking a bit embarrassed, returned with the check, I looked up at her confidently and said, "*Arigato gozaimasu,*" or "Thank you very much." I then continued pointing to the empty plate in front of me and said, "*Oishikatta desu,*" or "It tasted great."

She knew that I hadn't intended to eat the meat raw if I'd understood that a grill would come out, but she smiled widely and her whole posture relaxed as she giggled and said something, which I could tell meant that she was happy I liked it.

At least the total written on the bill was in standard numbers, so I was able to pay the correct amount. I put a few more Japanese *yen* on the tip than I would normally have. As I left, I said again, "*Arigato Gozaimasu. Oyasuminasai.*" Still smiling broadly, my charming waitress bowed formally and then waved as she said goodbye.

I walked out of the restaurant into the cool evening, proud that I hadn't spoken a word of English the entire time.

I was so charged up that I decided not to go home right away. I would stop by a local *izakaya* for another beer. I decided to go to one I'd never been to before, and I also decided that English was still off limits.

All was going well in the small bar until, while trying to compliment a mother with a little girl, I called the girl "*kowai,*" instead of "*kawaii.*" I learned from a hysterically laughing drunk Japanese guy that, with my nicest voice possible, I had said, "What a creepy little girl," instead of, "What a cute little girl." Although I had made it through an entire dinner without speaking any English, as I looked at the now confused mother in the *izakaya*, I realized that I still had a long way to go before I could claim to speak Japanese.

Your Turn to Explore

Have you ever made a mistake with a culture or language that you laugh about now? What was it?

Why is it better to go out and try your best to speak a language even if you make many mistakes?

Do Something Extraordinary: If you know someone from a different culture, learn a simple phrase in their native language and surprise them by saying it.

NINE

INSANE CHOICE

Washington State, USA; Paris, France. 1987–1994

I wasn't a very good student growing up. In fact, I was really bad, but something clicked during my junior year in high school. I really don't think there is a correlation, but it happened at about the same time that I tried mushrooms for the first time. Or maybe it was because I had some great teachers that year. Whatever the reason, something clicked, and I had a lot of catching up to do.

Up until that point, I remember reading a few elementary school books about Dick and Sally on some farm, and I remember something about frogs and toads that talked with each other, but that's about it. From kindergarten to eleventh grade I don't remember reading any other books except for Dungeons & Dragons manuals.

But, as I mentioned, something clicked, and after that click, I wanted to become a university professor, and a pedantic one at that. I didn't even care about the subject, but at that point, philosophy and psychology were the most exciting to me.

I began reading non-stop. I started devouring all the books that my smart friends had already read in their AP classes, and I enrolled in an extra early-morning class at Washington High School. I also enrolled in a psychology extension course at Pacific Lutheran University. When I wasn't studying or at football or hockey practice, I was reading. On weekends, I'd sometimes go through two or three books a day.

When my brother came back for Christmas break from Stanford University, he gave me a book. As I unwrapped *The Fountainhead* on Christmas morning, Mike said that it was a philosophy book.

I started reading the tiny-font 700-something-page book when a massive snowstorm delayed the January start of school. Fifty pages in, I started thinking to myself: *This isn't a philosophy book. What was Mike thinking? It is just a novel.* Then 250 pages in, I realized that Ayn Rand wasn't telling me philosophy like Hegel and Kant had done, but this book was making me *think* philosophy for myself.

As I realized this, I thought of Robert Persig and how he couldn't get his thoughts about Platonic and Aristotelian or classic versus romantic philosophy down on paper until he gave up the attempt and decided to write a book about a motorcycle trip across America with his son. The resulting classic *Zen and the Art of Motorcycle Maintenance* decanted his ideas, seamlessly expressing philosophical thoughts clearly on the pages of the novel.

The snow kept falling, and I kept reading. On that first day, I didn't take a single break. I wasn't rushing through the book. I was studying each line while also being totally caught up in the story of the novel. The second day, I continued reading until the afternoon when my mom asked me to go out and get more wood for the fireplace. I knew this wasn't going to be easy since I hadn't chopped any wood the prior weekend, as my parents had asked me to.

"Okay, Mom, I'll get it," I yelled into the other room, knowing that it would take a while. I put on white long johns, a brown flannel, and a hunting jacket and went out to get to work. When I first stepped outside, it was freezing with the snow coming down lightly at a good angle because of the wind. As I began splitting the large round wood sections into usable wedges, I warmed up immediately. Not only that, but I became tired more quickly than normal. That's when I realized that I hadn't eaten anything for over 24 hours.

Wow, I said to myself. *I can't believe I forgot to eat.*

As I thought this, my stomach growled as if on cue, but I was kind of excited about it. I'd had some water, but I hadn't eaten anything at all. I decided that since I already had a good start on a fast, I'd keep it up. I thought up a few self-imposed rules, which were that I would not eat any food, but I could drink water and a very limited amount of juice, but only regular things like orange or apple juice, and nothing thick or containing vegetables.

Excited to return to my book, I only chopped enough wood to get through the day and the next morning. When I went back into the house, I told my mom about how I hadn't eaten anything in almost two days and that I was going to keep it up. I don't think she was impressed, but she didn't say I shouldn't either.

After finishing *The Fountainhead*, I felt invigorated. I loved the book and decided to read everything Ayn Rand had ever written. I didn't know at the time how much that would be. As soon as I finished the book, I dated the top corner of the title page, which I did to each book I finished. I shelved the book with the others I had completed, which were kept separate from the books I had yet to read. I quickly selected another.

I read Freud next and then the silly fourth book in Douglas Adams' *Hitchhiker's Guide to the Galaxy* trilogy, and yes, I found it most amusing that there are four books, but we called it a "trilogy."

I spent most of my time reading on a couch facing the fireplace next to the large pane windows looking out over Hood Canal in Seabeck. (It was my only semester not at Washington High School, but at Central Kitsap.) However, every time I lifted my head for a moment, my eyes didn't go out the window, but fell on the gold and blue 14-volume *Encyclopedia of the Bible* set that my mom had gotten somewhere and which took up over two feet on the bookshelf next to the fireplace.

Maybe it was because I was becoming delirious from lack of food, but whatever the reason, after I finished *So Long, and Thanks for All the Fish*, I decided to start the encyclopedias. I made it through the entire first volume. It was now Saturday night. I had started my fast on the prior Monday evening. I had gone five full days without a single bite of food, and it felt wonderful.

My experience without food for five days was edifying. As already explained, I was so caught up in my first book that I didn't even think about it for the first two days. After I decided not to eat, I was fine for about an hour until I began thinking about it, and then I started feeling hungry. By far the worst was my third day. I felt really hungry during this time, and I felt a horrible taste in my mouth, which I found out at a later doctor visit was the buildup of natural poisons working their way out of my body. I had to brush my teeth every few hours. It started to feel like there was a piece of plastic in my mouth, and my teeth felt slippery. That part was strange.

It was the fourth and fifth days, though, when I stopped being hungry. The bad taste in my mouth subsided a bit, and although my body would become tired very quickly, gauged by my daily chore of splitting firewood, I felt alert mentally. I was certainly in a different state of awareness, and I enjoyed it. My body felt slow, but my mind became entirely focused and quick to grasp the things I was reading. The clarity surprised me, and I began to wonder what other things would send me to a more concentrated place such as this. I decided to explore more.

My exploration included experimenting with a few psychedelic drugs, and it wasn't just for recreation but out of curiosity about where the drugs could take me. I didn't do many, but one of my favorite things to do was to put a tab of LSD on my desk, lick my left index finger and place it on the acid. Then I'd write using my right hand. I have no idea if any of the acid really soaked into my skin as a few friends said it would, but I think the uncertain anticipation of what I was doing certainly put me in an unusual place. It never sent me to the amplified mental space, streaking naked through the cosmos, that a full tab of acid did, but I wrote many interesting things while doing this.

Other exploration included meditation. I read books on zen, mantras, sustained prayer, the third eye, chakras, and more, but mostly I created my own version where I'd sit with either my eyes open and loosely fixed on an object, or closed, attempting to have no thoughts whatsoever, but accepting whatever came. I had many strange experiences during these meditation practices, but one stood out.

I was sitting on the floor trying to get into a meditative state, but I was having difficulty. I couldn't not concentrate. I was on the floor in my room, and there was a corkboard on the floor about eight feet away. I was staring at an old newspaper clipping about Madonna's first concert ever which opened at the Paramount Theatre in Seattle.

At the start, my meditation did send me into a weird place. After only moments, the ceiling and the floor began to collapse into each other, creating a thin band of a squished image of the flattened wall, corkboard, and now a tiny sliver of a Madonna picture. Above and below the visual band was blackness. The horizontal band then turned to an angle and in a flash sailed away, leaving nothing, even though my eyes were open.

I was kind of curious about this "hallucination," but I blinked it off. Then I couldn't get back into it. I had only been sitting for a few minutes, and I struggled to get into a meditative place. Finally defeated by many distractions, I agitatedly gave up. When I stood and went to my desk to get a book, I was shocked. I looked at the clock, and it wasn't five minutes which had passed, but rather over two hours. The five-minute time period felt so real to me that it kind of scared me. I had to call my friend Kirk to talk myself down from the strange anxiety I was feeling from not understanding what had happened during the "missing" two hours. Although I was nervous, I began to think that all my playing with different levels of consciousness was beginning to be effective in allowing me to experience "reality" differently.

Sleep deprivation was another device I used to test the limits of my consciousness. About a week after the meditation episode, I intentionally didn't sleep for two days. I started on a Friday morning, and it was now late Saturday, or rather about two or three in the morning on Sunday. I'd read quite a bit that day, but at this point I was writing. In my mind, it was going to be my first philosophy treatise, but it was really nothing more than short chapters about my attitudes and ideas about emotions including love, hate, jealousy, fear, etc. I was totally feeling the effects of my lack of sleep, but the writing was somehow becoming easier and easier and faster and faster.

I almost always used a pencil rather than a pen or typewriter. I simply liked it better, and it became as if the pencil were writing itself, and I was just trying to keep up. I loved what was coming out of me and being produced in letters on the pages that kept going and going. I was on a roll, and I struggled to keep my hand moving as quickly as my thoughts. I began to tingle as this was happening, but I was not using any experimental drugs. I hadn't in weeks. Writing more and more, faster and faster, I marveled at what was being written, and finally I had to stop for a moment. My body was tense, and my fingers ached because of the pressure of the pencil. I also became aware that my neck was sore from being hunched over for so long. I finally looked up.

In my room, the foot of my bed was to my left, and my desk faced a large outside window. Because of the darkness outside and the light behind me, my window acted as a mirror, and I saw my reflection. As soon as my eyes connected with my image facing me, I heard a voice. The voice was in my head, but it very empirically felt like it was coming from outside of my thoughts, ulterior to my mind. The voice very clearly said: *You have two choices: put down the pencil and go to bed OR keep writing and become a genius.*

No other words were spoken, but it was absolutely clear that the implication was that if I kept writing and accepted the gift of genius, the consequence would be that I would also lose my ability to communicate with the outside world, with other people. The decision didn't even take a moment. The question felt real, and I felt not elation, but panic. Fear of insanity seized me. I immediately put my pencil down and crawled into my bed, but my fear didn't go away. I just lay there trying to sleep, but my mind was still racing. It took a very long time, but I finally succeeded in drifting off.

When I woke up the following morning, I still wasn't totally right. I felt disconnected. Even as I brushed my teeth, it was as if I were not totally in control of the line between my conscious and unconscious mind. I couldn't even drive a car because, although I was looking at one image at a time, it felt like I was seeing everything in two similar frames, which were about nine inches apart. My eyes told me that I was seeing one image, but not my brain.

Somehow from my perception, I was seeing two of everything. One image was clearly my conscious view, and the other was somehow less in my control as if it were a dream of which I wasn't 100 percent in charge.

On the following Monday, I went to school, but it was a blur. I tried to read, but I couldn't focus between the two realities that it felt like I was trying to negotiate. Writing was easier than reading, but nothing really productive seemed to be coming. Sleep wasn't a refuge, because I was lucid during it most of the time. I was aware that I was sleeping and dreaming, but I was also totally conscious and simply thought about what I wanted to do in my dream, but I wasn't released from the conscious portion of my brain. Two things I clearly remember doing while in my lucid dreams were swimming underwater (since I didn't need to breathe in my dream) and flying from my house on top of Golden Given Hill down to Tami Herskovitz's house and talking with her. I also spoke with Mary-Kate Olsen. Even though I knew I was only speaking with my self-created dream versions of Tami and Mary-Kate, for some reason, this was very comforting.

It took about a week to totally gain control of the line between my conscious and unconscious mind, but I still felt a bit off for about a month. I welcomed the gradual transformation back into having intentional rather than indiscriminate thoughts, but I began to wonder what would have happened if I had kept writing that night. A few years later, I told myself that if I were ever offered that choice again, I should probably take it.

Six years later, I would learn exactly what I would do if the question came up again. After graduating as an undergrad from UCLA, I went to Alaska to work for a bit and then moved to France. I was living in Paris writing an article for a French editor who lived in Rambouillet. I lived in a tiny "maid's quarters" room on the top floor (almost attic) of an old building in the fifteenth arrondissement. My cramped room had a low, angled ceiling, a small bed, a card table for a desk, and a tiny corner kitchen, which was nothing more than a small sink and hotplate, but from the detached bathroom, which I shared with four other rooms, I did have a view of the Eiffel Tower.

This small room became a magical place for me, and I began writing pages and pages of material. I had a Macintosh Classic computer and a lot of time. About five months into my seven-month stay in Paris, my writing began to take off. I was teaching English a few hours a day, training Muay Thai boxing once a day, reading existential philosophy, and the rest of the time, I'd write.

One evening I was on a roll, and I was particularly impressed with my writing. The next evening, I was even more excited about what was now appearing on the computer screen in front of me as my fingers scrambled to keep up with my thoughts. The next day was even better. That's when I recognized that the question might be asked of me again. I was getting close. My body started to have a similar surreal buzzing feeling as I'd had in my bedroom six years earlier. Just like the first time, absolutely no drugs or alcohol were involved, but I began to feel like my body was trying to catch up to my thoughts, but the gap was widening.

As my writing and the time with my thoughts continued to flow, I became vaguely aware that the question was getting nearer. It wasn't quite there though, and I could more pragmatically process what the answer to the question would mean. I became excited in many ways, but for the second time, it was an easy choice. I knew that I was too scared and that I would not have the courage to accept the proposition of isolated genius. Or would it simply be insanity?

I kept writing, and I was still impressed with what was happening, but I never again reached that strange place in my head where I released the reins of my thoughts and let them soar to a space beyond my regular mental capabilities—to that unchartered place well beyond the confined limits of the conscious part of my brain.

As I reflect on the repercussions of the offered question, I like to think that I made the right choice, but the curiosity of what really would have happened if I had chosen differently still lingers when I think about it. I was given a very unique choice, and although I'm happy with the person I am, having chosen one way, I'll never know what would have happened if I had selected differently. Unlike the brave protagonist in Robert Frost's "The Road Not Taken," I did not choose the road less traveled. As in Frost's poem, I doubt I'll ever be back standing before the diverging paths of that crazy choice again: to continue living on the edge or step off it.

Your Turn to Explore

Have you ever been faced with a decision that you felt would really change the direction of your life depending on the choice? What were the choices, and what did you decide?

What are ways we can become more in touch with our unconscious mind?

Do Something Extraordinary: Get in front of a mirror and set a timer for three minutes. Look into your own eyes, and begin by saying, "How is it going?" Then, just let your mind go where it will, but don't stop looking at yourself until the timer is up.

TEN

GUARDIAN ANGEL

Paris, France. 1995, 1988

I thought I might have heard something—a single strange, muffled, echoing boom—but I didn't think much of it. It might have just been my imagination. I was eating peaches on a small strip of grass outside the Shakespeare and Company bookstore in Paris. I wasn't at the famous English-language bookstore for literature; I just wanted to use the grass to sit on during my mini-picnic of three peaches. Other than the annoyance of a few too many French poodle droppings surrounding me, it was a very pleasant day.

Just prior to this short, enjoyable time, I had been walking down the underground tunnels leading to the platform for line B of the RER in the Métro de Saint-Michel station. While walking along the white-tiled pathway, I saw a vendor with a small makeshift table and some peaches resting on a flower-patterned pillowcase. I'd never purchased fruit or any other food in the metro tunnels before, and I wasn't even very hungry, but for some reason the peaches looked really good. Feeling somehow compelled, I bought three of them, turned around, and walked back out of the metro station, climbing the long stairs on my way out.

I didn't stay very long sitting in front of the bookstore. I casually ate two of the peaches, tossed the pits into a small green trash bin, and put the last one in my pocket. As I was walking along back toward the metro station, I licked my fingers and was just starting to wipe my hands on my pants when I rounded the corner near Le Départ Saint-Michel Café. That's when everything changed.

Smoke was billowing from the Saint-Michel Métro station, emergency crews were just arriving, and people were carrying bloody bodies out of the entrance to the station. In my shock, everything was silent. I could see people rushing out of the station, and I could see the flashing lights of the ambulances and police cars, which were speedily arriving, but I heard nothing. Then suddenly, as I focused on the face of a crying woman who was being carried out of the smoking station and set on a medical stretcher, the sound all came at once. The din was overwhelming.

If I thought I could have helped, I would have, but there were already many assisting. And professional firefighters and EMTs were arriving. I simply stood there with my mouth open as if I were watching a horrible scene in a movie. I stood for many, many minutes not knowing what to do. Finally, the smoke quit pouring out of the entrance, but bodies were still being loaded into ambulances, and people were still lying on the ground. There was nothing I could do, but I felt guilty about the thought of leaving.

When I finally forced myself to leave, I realized that I would have to walk to get to another metro station. The relatively short walk seemed to take hours, and I was trying to process what had happened. As I wondered if other trains would be running, I somehow felt ashamed for not being in the tragedy. I should have been there, but instead I'd bought three peaches and walked myself right out of the blast zone. I also felt somehow strange that I could just walk a few blocks to another metro and continue my life, and I was very thankful for that.

I learned later that it was a terrorist attack by radicalized Algerians who called themselves the Armed Islamic Group. I also learned that eight people died and 80 were maimed or injured.

***

Another shocking incident in my life also took place in Paris. This was about seven years prior to the 1995 Saint-Michel explosion. I use the term "shocking" very intentionally.

I was traveling around Europe for a few months. I also intentionally used the word "traveling," and not "backpacking." Because I used an old black snare drum case for my clothes and belongings, officially I didn't fit into the group of young "backpackers" who tramped around on EuRail passes. Essentially that is what I was. I'd bought the round case, which had a metal handle, at a pawn shop back in the United States, and I thought it was very cool.

The trip came to be after I graduated from high school and my grandmother took me to Norway to meet my relatives. I spent a few lovely weeks with my grandmother and my family meeting the aunts, uncles, and cousins that I didn't even know I had. After getting to know the extended family in Norway, my grandma returned to the US, and I headed south to explore Europe.

I don't even remember where I was coming from, but I do remember that I arrived in Paris during a massive rainstorm. It felt cold and wet even looking through the windows of the train. Water was blanketing the windows and coming down in sheets. When the train stopped at Gare de Lyon station, our train car was one of the farthest from the front. Passengers still had about 50 yards of open sky above us before reaching the massive stone and glass building of the station.

People were filing out of the train, walking fast or trotting toward the station along the platform and holding newspapers over their heads. I had just stepped off the train and took about five long steps when—BAM! It felt like someone hit me in the stomach full swing with a baseball bat.

At first, I didn't really know what had happened. I was standing hunched over in the rain about five feet from the train. My eyes immediately went totally black. Then everything turned blindingly white. As my eyes adjusted to normal, I could see an arc of electricity going from my hand, which was still gripping the drum case, to the train.

I just got struck by lightning, I said to myself, and I seemed to keep repeating, *Oh my gosh, oh my gosh* in my head as if in disbelief.

People were lying on the ground around me. Many were crying, and I wanted to cry as well. I desperately tried, but the wind was knocked out of me, so all I could do was stand there, still hunched, shocked, and begging for breath.

As people stood up, everyone was staring at me, stunned themselves. Finally, after a few moments, a man with grey hair, who must have been about 60 years old, started toward me. He wore grey slacks and a beige trench coat. He said something to me, but my ears were ringing. I couldn't hear him. He placed one hand on my elbow and his other hand on my back, and he began slowly guiding me down the platform toward the station.

The rain had let up a bit, but it was still very wet. Finally, I understood that the man was asking if I was okay. As my breath began to come back, I was able to straighten up a bit, and I nodded that I was okay. Once we were under the shelter of the large building, I tried to convince myself that I really *was* okay. The man left me and returned with a police officer who didn't speak any English, but he did his best to take over caring for me. The officer sat with me for a few minutes, and finally I nodded my head trying to smile and show that I was fine.

My right hand was still hurting. It strangely felt more like a bruise than a burn, and my head ached profoundly. I had never had a headache like this one. The headache returned each day for four days at 4:00 pm, the exact time when I was struck, but I was otherwise fine. I spoke with many people about what had happened, and most agreed that again it seemed the angel looking out for me showed up in time for this incident just like the many other times in my life where things could have turned out horribly different.

Your Turn to Explore

Have you ever nearly escaped something very bad happening? What happened, and did it change the way you think about your life?

If you should die tomorrow, would you consider that you lived a good life, or would you have done anything differently?

Do Something Extraordinary: Imagine that you were going to die in one week. Next, think of anyone to whom you would like to say something before you are gone. Now, find them and say it.

ELEVEN

LION'S DEN

Los Angeles, USA. 2004. Thirty-Four Years Old

It was about 11:00 pm. My motorcycle jolted up and down over the uneven concrete slabs. I felt like every car I passed knew where I was going.

After seeing the exit from the freeway, I leaned onto the ramp and was greeted by two LAPD cruisers with lights flashing. Turning left, I saw that they were backed up by another duo at the next intersection. Turning right, I saw two more and became aware of the ghetto bird, or police helicopter, circling above.

As one of the cops pulled through a red light to tail me, I became suddenly aware of how illegal my chopper was with no turn signals, no horn, no front fender, and ape hangers above my head. What they couldn't see was the notched knife blade that served as my oil dipstick. After many minutes and many turns in this frightening concrete neighborhood, the cop—who must have realized that the only legal thing about my bike was that it wasn't stolen—left me.

Now after taking 20 weird turns to get rid of the cop, I found myself completely lost. I telephoned AK for directions.

As I pulled up, AK stood tall in his colors. He pointed to a few choppers and said I could park in front of them because their owners were sure to stay all night. After a bear hug and a hearty slap on the shoulder, AK told me that the guys I would meet knew of me as the "Harley rental guy and martial arts expert." Great, just what I needed!

We walked up to an eight-foot-high barbed fence with six giant, leather-vested, tattooed club members guarding it. AK asked if I had any weapons, which I didn't due to his request that I not bring any. I was frisked all over. There were indeed no secrets left between me and the giant guard. As we walked deeper into the compound, my friend asked if the guard had grabbed my balls, a question to which I responded with a curt affirmative.

AK responded simply, "Good, he's supposed to be thorough."

After passing the heavily guarded narrow opening of the towering iron gate, police were suddenly non-significant. I'd entered the lair of a notorious outlaw motorcycle club. We passed hundreds of bikes and neared a large circus-sized tent leading to the entrance of the clubhouse, a warehouse at the end of a non-lit industrial park bordered by two crossing freeways. The sound of cars was silenced by the growing din of excited bikers and the distant thumping of helicopter blades in the dark sky.

While entering the clubhouse, AK introduced me to the president and sergeant at arms as well as others from his chapter. There existed several chapters at the party. He also told me to get a club T-shirt, which he encouraged me to don as quickly as possible.

After a few beers and many handshakes, I began to feel at ease. The men with barbarian tattoos on their faces no longer seemed as frightening, and I even started to realize the appeal.

Not only was the brotherhood comforting, but I liked the idea that every man in the house was defined by circumstances outside of society and was fully responsible for all his actions. Laws and social norms protect nobody within the boundaries of the clubhouse. It was personally exciting to be defined by only two things: first, my acceptance to enter the clubhouse and, second, my actions within.

As an outsider, I was twice tested by individuals who were simply checking whether I belonged or not. The first was a bit rattling. I had entered a long conversation with a club member, talking about girls and relationships. Then after about 15 minutes, I realized that he was no longer together with the wife he had been talking about. So, I asked, "Oh, so you're no longer together?"

"Do you want me to rub you out?" he mumbled.

"What?" I responded.

His entire body language changed immediately. He asked, "Are you fucking begging me to kill you?"

I had gotten too personal, too quickly.

His posture morphed, and he became the Incredible Hulk before my eyes as he leaned toward me with fists clenched. I could tell that he was about to charge, and I imagined how I would let him come at me—*fall backward as I grab him and attempt to roll on top of him*—but in any case, me getting into a fight in this place would be entirely perilous.

Thinking quickly, I finally said, "I'm sorry, man, I'm just trying to learn from someone who knows more than me," and I reached out my hand for an interlocking fist handshake.

He reciprocated the handshake, but still looked agitated, so panicking, I said, "Let's change the subject." I pointed to one of his tattoos and asked, "What is this tattoo on your neck?"

Maybe not the best way to get out of a bad situation—especially when not getting too personal too fast seemed imperative—but it worked.

The second test was entirely different. After being more comfortable in the clubhouse, I was heading to the bar at the other end of the house when I felt a formidable slap on the top of my right shoulder. I turned around to see a six-foot-five monster with two mirroring AK-47 machine guns tattooed on each side of his neck with the barrels pointing diagonally up just above his Adam's apple. He was with two cronies, and the three of them stared meanly at me.

I looked back at the big, tall guy in the center with calm, even eyes, which were neither provoking nor scared.

He wanted a reaction. If I looked aggressive, he would have loved to have proven his mettle once again by tearing me apart in front of his friends. If I looked scared, he would have loved to have chased me out of the clubhouse.

I remained neutral.

After a few seconds, which seemed like a long time, he smiled, extended his hand, and asked, "Hey, how is it going? Are you having a good time? Can I get you a beer?" He walked with me to the bar and handed me a beer.

Seemingly having passed the tests both times, the individuals offered warm, strong handshakes and welcomed me into their world.

I stayed through most of the night. As the sky was just starting to get light, I was given motherly advice on how to avoid any remaining policemen when I left. As I fired up the monster, my adrenaline was still in excess. I felt like doing a nice, long burnout but realized that such a show was unnecessary in this crowd on this morning.

I stepped the bike into first gear and calmly pulled out.

Your Turn to Explore

Have you ever been surrounded by a group or individual who totally intimidated you? Who was it, and why were they intimidating?

What can we gain by spending time with people different from us?

Do Something Extraordinary: Get out of your comfort zone and start a conversation with someone totally different from you.

TWELVE

THURSDAY NIGHT IN BANGKOK

Bangkok, Thailand. 1997. Twenty-Seven Years Old

D is for drugs, danger, delirium, delight.

A toilet in a room, a ceramic bowl containing floating vomit, and two logs from a ponderous red-eyed fool who can only repeat the lyrics of a catchy tune, "I Want to Go Higher," with "higher" actually meaning "lower" because the addition of more chemicals to an already saturated body could do nothing other than cause the fool—in this case, me—to gravitate toward the stench of the digested noodle-curry soup.

"I Want to Go Higher" rang in my ears as tears beaded in my eyes.

Too much? I questioned.

With an index finger, I attempted to expel the residue of drugs long since integrated into my tissue.

Feeling the cold heat of nausea bead on my brow, I waited, but nothing came. Further and deeper the finger went, feeling the trachea deep at the bottom of the throat. Coughing and gagging, a small rush of acidified bright yellow juice from within my intestines squirted and ran down my hand into the toilet.

Melodically, "I Want to Go Higher" rang in my ears.

QUIET! The neighbors are listening. They know … How many times have I heard them sick and screaming into the ceramic bowl?

Stand up slowly. Rinse off your hand with running water, I think to myself.

The loud gurgle of water entering old pipes filled the room. I dried off with a dirty towel and looked in the mirror.

Is that me? I asked.

Red was the overall color of my face. Eyes were black saucers surrounded by blood-red whites. The smile was both of excitement and regret. A switchblade night will do that to a person. Loads of amphetamines capped off with a snort of ketamine offered from the hand of a notorious Bangkok pharmacist whose night job entailed owning a dance club.

***

Earlier in the evening, I had stopped by a few times checking to see if he was at his club. Not there, I returned to another less-intense hangout near Sukhumvit Soi 4, but I couldn't stay away.

When I finally located him, I was in the in-between. I danced intentionally. It wasn't until later that the music entered my nervous system, and I became a willing cog in an enormous machine of pleasure. Tranced, I'd say I was.

It was a moment when the trance was broken that the doctor asked me to follow him out of the club and into the café next door. Through the red lamp-lit room lined with velvet red couches, we entered the bathroom together and locked the door. Dr. Pharmacy started unfolding a red 100 baht note.

"K?" I asked.

"Yeah."

"Do you have any heroine?"

"No."

He held out a key with a large white mound balanced on its end.

"Half," I said in a weak attempt at calming my conscience.

He held the key to my nostril, and—*sniff!*—a magic trick made it disappear.

I turned to the urinal, unzipped my trousers, and pissed. Behind me, I was aware of the doctor's own magic act making the white powder disappear.

Nervous, oh so nervous I was as we walked unchecked back into the crowded club. Anticipating the drug, I forgot about the doctor and headed for the dance floor. The music was making sense. It touched not only my nervous system because of the amphetamines, but now it began to touch the echo of my existence—that unspeakable void, which lends us the ability to communicate with the outside world. The music bypassed my immediate consciousness and even my unconscious dreams by speaking directly to the envoy, that strange voice, ulterior to the self, that tells us at any given instant what to speak and even think. I danced not only of my own accord but as directed.

***

After telling my story to the toilet, I drank fervently from a warm plastic container of water. It flowed smoothly down my damaged throat. Lying naked on top of my sheets, I found neither the desire nor capability to sleep.

I floated, tranquilized. I could see my body from above:

His eyes wide open—very wide. His body relaxed, pulsed with energy. The tune, "I Want to Go Higher," was not in his ears because he could not be concerned with such trivial matters. He existed and was content. It felt so good. The imagination took control, and he became a horse, a tranquilized and paralyzed horse, who floated on the waves of reality, dreaming that he was awake, with wide-open eyes—not dreaming though—feeling.

He never fell asleep.

* * *

The clock read 8:03 am. The metal wire fan turned languidly.

I opened my eyes, moved comfortably, and smiled at the somewhat cool morning. I climbed out of bed, wet with sweat, and stepped into the shower to cleanse the outside of my contaminated body before starting my day. I felt relieved that the night was over, but I dreaded the day. I would get through it with no idea how dangerously close to addiction I was becoming. Pulled toward the gravity of the surreal, I wanted more, and that was the difference between the occasional transcendental deep dive into my mind and the mundane stupidity that was becoming a habit.

Thank God I caught what was happening before slipping out of myself forever.

Your Turn to Explore

Have you ever become close to or struggled with addiction? If so, how did it manifest—alcohol, drugs, gambling, shopping, eating, something else? Where are you with it currently?

What are the main reasons people become addicted to anything?

Do Something Extraordinary: If you struggle with addiction, get help right away. Call someone, tell someone, and get your life back. If you don't struggle, think of someone you know who might. And see if there is any respectful way you can help them.

THIRTEEN

FIGHTING

Washington State, USA. 1972–1994

I lost the first fight in my life. I was barely three years old and at a public park with monkey bars, a play structure, and lots of sand. My opponent was also about three years old. I had never met him before, but the blond, baby-faced kid threw some sand at me. I told him to stop, but he did it again, this time getting sand in my eyes, and he was going for more.

I went over to him and tried to wrestle the sand from his fist. Then we began awkwardly grappling around in the sand until his arm was around my neck from behind. I was stuck.

I couldn't move at all, so I started to cry. He let me go, and I ran over to my mom who was about 50 feet away talking to some- one, probably the kid's mom since we were the only ones there. I was so young that I didn't even know how to explain what had happened, so I just cried and pointed. Even at three, I hated the feeling of being controlled like that, and I told myself that if anyone picked on me like that again, I'd do more to avoid losing the fight.

Not only did I want to avoid being bullied myself, I kind of took it on myself to protect others from being bullied. I was generally very soft spoken, but I was pretty stocky for my age in elementary school, and I ended up sticking up for people quite often.

***

I first saw the shoes in a department store. My mom and I were looking for something to replace the thrashed and uncomfortably small shoes I had been wearing for way too long. After getting my feet measured on the little movable metal foot-sizing tool, I tried on many ugly practical shoes that my mom and the cute lady working at the store had selected. I giggled every time the lady helped wiggle my feet into a new pair of stiff shoes, none of which I liked.

Then I saw them from across the aisle as if they were calling to me. The low-top, black Nikes were awesome. I hopped off the orange vinyl bench, walked over, and showed my mom.

"Definitely not," my mom said.

"Why?" I asked in a high voice, already preparing to beg.

"First," my mom continued, "I don't like them, and second, they are way too expensive."

I knew that the chances of me getting the shoes were slim, but I made my argument that they would last longer than the other cheaper shoes and that I'd take the best care of them ever. I even vowed not to let them touch dirt or grass.

My mom's decision to get the Nikes wasn't quick, but in the end, I got them.

I upheld my promise to avoid dirt and grass in the shoes for a full two weeks. I even limited school recess to basketball, tetherball, and four square on the pavement. I forewent kickball and tackle football with the friends I usually played with on the field.

Then one day a fourth grader was making fun of Tang on the blacktop path along the side of the baseball field.

"Stop," I said to the older, aggressive kid who was teasing Tang about his name being the same as the powdery orange drink mixture. The kid continued and added physical taunting to his game.

"You better stop," I said again.

Then the kid started bringing Tang's limited English and tan skin into the bullying. Next, he pushed Tang, telling him to "go back to Cambodia."

At this point, I stepped in between the bully and Tang.

The bully backed off the blacktop. I stopped. He was only about three feet away, and I looked down at the invisible barrier between the blacktop and the wet grass.

The kid noticed, calling, "Ha, ha, you can't get me."

His taunting of Tang became worse and worse. He hopped around now about ten feet away. If he were only taunting me, I could have walked away, but he was going back and forth between insulting me and spewing vicious words at Tang, who just stood there, trying not to cry.

Finally, I decided that my promise should be broken. I ran into the grass. It took about halfway across the baseball outfield for me to catch the bully, but I did. It was his turn to cry.

Afterwards, I felt horrible. I didn't feel horrible that I beat up the bully because that was justice, but I was genuinely sad that my shoes were dirty. I tried to clean them as best I could, but without much benefit.

When I got home that day, I told my mom what had happened.

She wasn't even angry. She said that she was proud that I had done well keeping the shoes clean over the past few weeks and that she would understand if I wanted to play on the grass with them going forward. In a funny way, I think she was saying that even though she didn't condone fighting, I should support people like Tang on or off the pavement.

***

In elementary school, most of the fights I got into weren't horribly violent. One that could have been nasty was with Ken Donaldson. Ken was one of the few black kids in our school, and he was both fast and strong. We were on the outside basketball court during recess, and it was accusations of fouls that led to the conflict.

During the fight, as I was moving up and down in a Mohammed Ali-type boxing style, Ken made a keen observation.

"You a jellybean," Ken said, as I bounced up and down in my boxing stance.

I was taken off-guard by the random comment.

"You a white hoppin' jellybean," Ken said again, right as I was going in to punch him.

We had already each taken a few good blows. As I made to hit Ken, he grabbed me. He was ready to throw me onto the asphalt, but we both found ourselves laughing so hard about what he had said.

Amidst my own chuckling, I managed to yell out, "Stop!"

Ken, laughing himself, stopped.

We hugged for a few more seconds making sure that the other guy wouldn't start up again, and then we were instantly back to being friends.

***

Probably the craziest timing for a childhood fight was during a school Christmas singing performance. Some kid named Terry and I weren't getting along for some reason, and during the performance, we were placed next to each other on the top row of the small stadium that we were standing on. I felt he was too close to me, and he felt I was too close to him.

As our class was singing "Away in a Manger," we began shoving each other with our feet to get space, but it wasn't working. He put his hand on my stomach and pushed me backward. As I was falling backward off the three-foot stage, I pulled him with me. We fell together and immediately began wrestling around on the floor behind the singers.

A teacher quickly grabbed us, walked us behind a curtain out of the multi-purpose room and across the breezeway into the principal's office. She shut the door and left us there while she went to get the principal.

That was a dumb idea.

We looked at each other and were immediately locked in battle again. First, we fell into the desk, then it moved to a filing cabinet, then a bookshelf. We were struggling on the floor when Mr. Ponzer walked in.

"Stop!" Mr. Ponzer shouted loudly and angrily. "What in the world are you doing?" he shouted again.

Terry and I just looked up at him from our floor position. There were papers all over the room.

"Now you've done it," Mr. Ponzer muttered as he walked around his desk.

He opened the bottom drawer.

Not everyone at Elmhurst Elementary School had been spanked by the principal, but everyone did know where his paddle was kept. It was legendary, that paddle—about two feet long, four inches wide, and lore was that it had holes drilled into it to sting even more.

Normally, it took three visits to the principal's office before the paddle would come out, but not this time.

Mr. Ponzer pulled it out and slammed the door closed. We could tell that he was being more than an "objective executor of punishment" at this moment. He was extremely angry.

Wielding the paddle up in the air, he yelled about how serious the incident was. "How could you do this during a school event? How could you trash my office?" he hollered.

While starting to yell out the question, "Who's first?" in order to show how hard he was going to spank us, he whacked his wooden desk with the paddle. It snapped off at the handle. The thick part of the paddle went flying. Mr. Ponzer's eyes went comically wide as he looked at the stub of the handle left in his hand.

Though Terry and I were totally frightened, in response to this unexpected turn of events, we both seemed to be choking back laughter. We were desperately trying to contain our giggles, but it was not possible.

I think, at this point, Mr. Ponzer realized how close to dangerously out of control he himself was, so he just pointed to the door and yelled, "Get out!"

It took us no time at all to scramble out the door.

It was never brought up again.

***

One of my worst moments during a fight was when my mom helped someone beat me up. Yep, you read that correctly. My loving mom helped someone beat me up.

It started with me and Bill Bailey playing in my front yard. I spent tons of time playing with Bill because he lived close. We were great friends even though he was a few years younger than me.

One day, for whatever reason kids start to fight, Bill and I had a fight. Although Bill was really tough, he was still younger than me, and I got him, at least this time.

A few minutes after the fight, I saw Sam Bailey through my living room window. He was angrily storming across the yard, heading to my house. I knew what to expect. Now the tables were turned.

As any good older brother should, Sam was not about to let his little brother get beat up by someone older than him. Sam was older than me, but only by a year, and I had made it fair game.

As Sam charged up my front porch, I opened the front door ready to fight. It was a vicious exchange of blows. I'd like to say I was winning, but we were just exchanging powerful shots equally until my mom rushed into the entryway.

She must have been yelling, "Stop!" but we were full on at it, so my mom grabbed both of my elbows from behind, pulling them back, and totally exposed my stomach.

I saw it coming in slow motion, and there was nothing I could do.

Sam saw the opportunity and took it. He hit me squarely in the stomach very hard, and the wind was immediately knocked out of me. Sam knew there was nothing more he needed to do. Revenge had been served, so he ran out the door and went home.

I didn't mind losing the fight as much as I did mind that my mom helped. In the end, within two days, my mom had been forgiven, Bill and I were back to playing in the front yard, and Sam and I were friends again.

***

In another string of sibling revenge encounters, I almost had to fight an entire family.

The first fight took place just after music class as we were walking back to our main classroom. As we were lining up to leave the music room, Leonard, one of my classmates, was meanly cutting in line in front of a smaller kid. Leonard started elbowing the smaller kid in the stomach to get in front.

The smaller kid tried to hold his own but ended up welling with tears as he conceded the position in line. I could tell that it was less about Leonard wanting to be near the front of the line as it was about being mean to the smaller kid.

The substitute music teacher didn't seem to care, but I did. As soon as we were outside, I taught Leonard a quick lesson in politeness. The fight was swift, probably more embarrassing than hurtful to Leonard. If Leonard felt he could elbow a small kid in the stomach, I felt I could do something to him in return.

It should have been easy to figure out—when Leonard's brother came after me as I was walking home from school—that his brother wouldn't have more success because his brother was his identical twin. We were all the same age. They were both taller than me, but also much thinner. The second fight was also quick.

Then, it was time for the big guns to come out: Joe, their older brother, older than all of us by at least three years. Joe found me alone the next morning getting ready for my Saturday paper route. I was putting the inserts into the newspapers next to the large wooden blue drop-off box when Joe came swiftly riding his ten-speed towards me.

Joe was not only much older than me, he was also much taller. The bike crashed as he jumped off it. The angry Joe charged, but I ended up tearing him apart. I hit him quite a few times. He tackled me. I hit him more while we rolled around on the wet green morning grass. I had taken a few good hits to the face, but after a while it was obvious to both of us that no matter what Joe tried, he wasn't going to get me. The fight with Joe was actually a pretty big one because he kept coming after me long after the fight should have been over. His injuries were superficial, but he certainly had two black eyes and a bloody nose.

Later that day, while I was raking grass in my front lawn, a red and white pick-up truck tore into my driveway. Joe was sitting in the passenger seat, and Joe's dad hastily jumped out of the truck. "Look what you've done, you little bastard!" he yelled viciously. "I can't believe you beat him up!"

I was stunned and very frightened.

My parents weren't home, and Joe's dad started walking toward me. He was carrying a stick. "I should beat *you* up," he spit, and the look in his eyes showed that he just might. "I should show you what it feels like, you little punk," he continued getting right up above me.

I was probably 12 years old, and this very agitated adult was threatening me. I wanted to cry, but I held it back as much as I could.

"He attacked me," I said pleadingly, and then the tears started coming down my face.

Joe's dad didn't look concerned at all. He did stop though, and he angrily walked back to the truck. I looked at Joe sitting in the truck and actually felt bad for him that he had been beaten up by someone almost four years younger and six inches shorter. This was different from when Sam wanted to stick up for his brother because of the vast age difference between Joe and me. The whole thing just felt unfortunate. Unlike most of the other altercations with kids my own age, Joe and I would never be friends, so there was never any closure.

***

Very different from the unfortunate fight with Joe, one notable fight that took place on the other side of my yard was with Jay Kyzenski. I learned a good lesson from this episode.

Jay was quite a bit smaller than I was, but everyone knew that he had been practicing karate for a few years and was thought to be very good at it. Jay and I were friends, and I can't even remember why we had arranged to fight. Maybe it was because I felt threatened by the mystery of his karate skills. Either way, we agreed to fight at the top of Golden Given Hill just up the road from the Mayfair and Brookdale Road bus stop.

I had gotten to the top of the hill first. Barry Conner, who was a few years older, walked up the hill with Jay. Barry was going to act kind of like the mediator for the set-up fight. We met in a small grassy area right off the side of the road.

"Okay, let's go," I said to Jay, putting my hands up.

Jay had brown feathered hair. He just stood relaxed. He looked at me and said, "I can't fight you unless you hit me first."

"That is stupid," I said. "Let's fight."

Jay repeated that he wouldn't unless I hit him, so I slowly reached out my fist and tapped him softly in the chest.

"That doesn't count," Jay said, "It has to be a real hit."

Just as Jay didn't feel right fighting unless he was hit first, I didn't feel comfortable hitting him in his unprotected face as he stood with his hands down by his sides. Finally, I wound up and punched him very hard on his left arm, almost by his shoulder.

It was a powerful blow, but as soon as it happened, I saw a white flash. Before my punching fist was even back to my guard, Jay had hit me in the face very, very fast and very hard. My head snapped back, and I charged in, wrestling Jay to the ground until he couldn't move. He said, "Okay, it's over."

The fight was only about 20 seconds, and as soon as it was over, Jay left. I asked Barry who had won the fight, and he said, "Well, officially you did because Jay said to stop, but you are going to have a pretty nasty black eye for a while."

As Jay walked down the hill, I felt kind of bad. I was hurt worse than him, but I respected him. I had also learned a lot from him about honor. Remembering Jay's ethic about not fighting unless really provoked stayed with me for a very long time.

***

It was in ice hockey that I began to enjoy the sport-side of fighting. Mark McGuire, whom we called "Killer," and I ended up being among the enforcers of our hockey team. The official name for our team was the Tacoma Rangers, but our unofficial name was the Tacoma Bitch Killers. We weren't the most skilled team, but we certainly were one of the toughest. Our team yell before games was, "They've got the skill, but we've got the will." We were kind of like the Bad News Bears of ice hockey even though it was Junior B level and most players were between 16 and 20 years old. That didn't stop our first shot of every game being an intimidating slap shot toward the goalie's face. We ended up with an over 50 percent winning season mostly because a lot of teams feared us, but that is part of hockey.

One guy who wasn't scared was the defensive player opposite me on the Portland Blackhawks, our main rival. I played right defense in my blue and orange uniform, and he played left in his red and black colors. He was one of the enforcers of his team, and he was also much larger than most other players. We played the Blackhawks often, and he and I started really building up a grudge. We knew that it was going to come to a fight at one point, but it didn't have to.

During a Saturday afternoon game at Sprinker Ice Rink in Spanaway, we were playing Portland. It was a rough and intense game, and emotions were beginning to boil. That is when it happened. After a weird block on the other team's goal, the puck bounced out to center ice. I was still near my goal, and the enforcer was by his goal, and the puck was right between us with no one around. Our eyes met for a moment from across ice, and we both began charging at full speed toward the puck. About half-way there, I think we each realized that neither of us cared about the puck, and we collided head on into each other like two bulls.

Everything went totally blank. There was a big white flash, and then after a few moments when I could see and think again,

I was standing like a tripod with my skates wide and leaning onto my hockey stick for support to stay up. Looking down, I saw blood dripping from my face and landing right on the chest of the jersey of my opponent who was lying on his back between my legs. My helmet was long gone. It had smashed down, breaking my nose before flying off ahead of me. Luckily, I was right next to the boards in front of my bench because I was still shaken and wobbly. I dove to the boards, and my teammates helped pull me over the short wall and onto the bench. With all the great moments of hockey, that is probably my favorite.

***

It was hockey that got me into boxing. I first started boxing at Fort Lewis Army Base with Tommy Mooney. He had already begun training there, and I was stoked to begin.

We trained at McVeigh Gym, and the coach was an old Puerto Rican soldier with a strong accent and a way with words. The first thing he did when he met me was push firmly on my nose with his thumb. The very first thing he said to me was that my nose was too sturdy and was going to get broken. Then he said in a horribly funny accent, "And ya have to wear da slippers in da shower. Dey is lot a pubic hairs around here."

He was a great coach, but I was limited to boxing only when Tommy could go because we had to have a military ID to get onto base. One day, Tommy didn't have the vehicle ID pass, so I asked another friend if Tommy and I could borrow his car, which had the needed sticker because his dad worked on the base.

On the way, as I was turning left onto 112th from Golden Given Road, a car slammed into the right front corner of the car. Tommy was a tough dude, and he proved it in the accident. We never wore seatbelts, and Tommy's head punched a bubble into the front windshield. When he flew back into his seat, Tommy simply looked at me with a bloody forehead and said, "Dang, the window broke." Just like that. He didn't say anything about his head hurting, just that the window broke. Other than the whole car being totaled, we were okay, but that did end our boxing career together.

Finally, I made it to martial arts. I trained a bit of ninjutsu during my first few years of college. Then at UCLA, I was turned on to Jeet Kune Do (JKD) or "the way of the intercepting fist." This is the art created by Bruce Lee, and it opened my eyes to the concept: "Learn everything, absorb what is useful, and get rid of what doesn't work for you." I first trained with Sifu Burton Richardson in a rec class at Wooden Center. Then I also began training with Sifu Dan Inosanto who was Burton's teacher as well as the senior student, protégé, and best friend of Bruce Lee.

We trained all kinds of things, but the nervous system training was one of the things I liked best. We'd practice sensitivity drills with a partner, with a combination of soft punches, elbows, and blocks. Then we'd do this with the lights off to really feel the movements of an opponent and the physics of movements without having to think about them. We also did exercises where we'd be startled and have to react as quickly as possible to an unknown surprise. This really played a role years later when I was attacked at a bowling alley in Washington, an incident I'll soon explain.

After finishing university, I moved to Alaska to do construction for the summer. I lived in remote Eagle River, but that didn't stop me from wanting to continue martial arts. I found a school teaching Ed Parker's American Kenpo Karate. It was all the way down in Anchorage about an hour away. I'd heard that Ed Parker's Kenpo was extremely tough and effective, so I decided to join. When I filled out the forms on the application to train, in my youthful enthusiasm about all the things I had trained, I wrote all the various teachers I'd had in ninjutsu, Jeet Kune Do, Muay Thai, boxing, etc. I really wasn't trying to show how good I thought I was, but I think my training list made the wrong impression on the instructor.

The first part of the two-hour class, on that first day, was awesome. I loved what we were learning, and it was intense. Then came the sparring. It wasn't full contact, but we did have open-finger padded gloves and shin guards. There were various levels of expertise in the room, but I was winning against almost all the opponents put in front of me as we rotated around the room exchanging partners about every five minutes. I was exceptionally happy that I was holding my own against one of the higher belts who was also a bit larger than me. That's when I think the instructor/owner of the school thought that I needed to be humbled.

The instructor intentionally switched places, and it was time for me to spar with him for the last session of the day. At first it started okay, but it quickly began getting more and more intense. And then it became absolutely brutal. I left my first day of class with a ripped shirt, bloody nose, and a loose tooth. All of this, and I know that the instructor was still significantly holding himself back. In the end, it took the instructor about two weeks to learn that my excitement for training was way larger than my ego. We began to get along great, and I learned a lot from him over the next two summers.

After Alaska, I was visiting my home in Washington State when one night, Dean Crowley, a few new friends, and I went dancing at a club called The Back 40. After that, we ended up at a bowling alley. One of the two girls we were with knew the bouncer who we learned was named Mark. Mark had a crush on her, and he evidently didn't like that she was with other guys, even though we were just friends and nothing more. We drank some beer, and the barmaid would come by every so often and give us mixed drinks, just because she liked us. We were having a blast but finally were told by the bouncer that the bar was closing.

Taking our time, we gathered our things still laughing amongst ourselves and began walking out with the bouncer agitatedly walking behind us. Then I remembered the barmaid, so I turned around, leaned around the bouncer and waved to the barmaid and said, "Bye, see you next time, and thanks again." She waved back.

Immediately the bouncer got right in my face. "It's two o'clock. Get the fuck out," he said viciously.

I was in a great mood, and I said, "Listen, I'm ten feet from the front door. I'm going to turn around and walk away, and—"

I was going to continue, "And you just do the same," but I didn't get that far. He violently head-butted me squarely in the face.

I can only tell you what happened next because Dean and the two girls I was with told me. After the head-butt, the bouncer began throwing punches at my head. I still don't remember it, but they said he threw at least three bombs directly at my face, and I dodged and parried all of them even though, because of the head-butt, my brain was essentially out. No one was home.

Then I came back. It was as if a lightbulb went on in my head, and I said to myself, *Oh my gosh, I'm in a fight.*

At the same time, I realized this, Dean charged in. The bouncer hit him rapidly three times in the head and temple. Then he came at me again. I dodged one more punch, then punched him with my left hand and then right, and then put him in a tight headlock. At this point, I thought we had control and that the fight would be over, but he reached up and grabbed my bottom lip and ripped it down tearing the septum connecting the front of my face to my lower gums.

With the jolt of pain, I was still in a good position and I actually said to myself, *Don't hurt him too much,* as I punched him four times with my left hand right into his face ,which was tightly held between my right elbow and stomach.

As soon as I hit him, he went limp, and at this point I knew it was over. I then said to the crowd of people who were watching, "Listen, I don't want to fight. I'm good. I'm going to let him go." As I said this, I released my grip, and he fell unconscious to the floor.

Dean, the two girls, and I quickly walked out the front glass doors. When we got to the car, I thanked Dean for jumping into the fight, and I began assessing the three golf-ball-sized knots on his head from the blows he had taken. I was proud of the way he had charged in to help. As I was getting into the car, I realized that my wallet had fallen out during the fight.

"Don't go back in there," one of the girls pleaded.

"Don't worry," I responded, "I'm not looking for more trouble, but I don't want to lose my wallet either." When I walked back in, I picked up my wallet from the bloody floor. The bouncer was still unconscious with people hovering over him.

From the unexpected head-butt, my nose was bleeding, and all my top front teeth felt loose. The inside of my lip was still torn, but otherwise I was fine. When I was dropped off at my house, my adrenaline was still pumping, so I ran downstairs to wake up Matt, a college student who was living with us.

"Matt," I said, waking him up, "I just got into a fight."

"What?" Matt said as he sat up in bed. When he saw me, his eyes went wide.

"Erik," he said in shock. "Are you okay? Look at all that blood." I was wearing a blue denim shirt and khaki pants, and there was blood from my armpit to my socks—lots of it.

"Oh my gosh," I said, horrified myself at how much blood there was. I was coated in it. I began to panic that I had indeed hurt the bouncer too much. I wondered if he could have died.

Immediately, I ran back upstairs into the kitchen and frantically dug the phone book out of the top drawer near the yellow phone on the wall. I called the bowling alley. I acted like I was a friend of Mark's who heard he had gotten into a fight, and I asked how he was. They told me that he had broken his nose but was otherwise okay. I was relieved that he was okay, and I heard later that he not only broke his nose, the management of the bowling alley saw the fight, and he was fired for starting it. Additionally, he was demerited in the military for starting a fight with a civilian. Again, I was glad he wasn't hurt worse, but I'm happy he got beat up. In a fashion entirely different from Jay Kyzenski, this guy had no respect or honor in a fight, and he got what he deserved.

Reflecting on my schoolyard scuffles, I'm kind of glad they happened. No one was ever seriously hurt and hopefully a few kids even learned a good lesson about treating people better. As I got older, I'm happy that in all the years that I was involved with combative sports, I really never looked for fights. I always liked to say that I was the last person to look for a fight, but one of the first to respond to idiots looking for trouble.

Being around a lot of intense people throughout my life, I sometimes think the world would be a better place if more people simply lived by a simple adage popularized by the Hells Angels: *You treat me good, and I'll treat you better. But if you treat me bad, I'll fuck you up.* Or even better, maybe we could at least adhere to the Golden Rule: *Treat others how you want to be treated.*

Your Turn to Explore

Which is more important: physical strength or intelligence? Has it always been this way?

Think of your very favorite moment while doing sports, music, or another interest of yours. What happened, and how did it make you feel?

Do Something Extraordinary: The prior story highlighting fights from my life is culturally outdated. Fights growing up were common and not that big of a deal. I think in some ways we kids in the '70s gained from these competitions. What are some ways modern-day children can learn valuable lessons about anger, cooperation, and resolving conflict? If you have kids, talk with them about something that was common during your younger life that is now uncommon. A conversation about bullying might not be a bad idea either.

FOURTEEN

PLAYING WITH KNIVES

USA, Africa, Europe. 1989–2001

It was getting dark. I was near the outskirts of Oran in Algeria. I was under an overpass near the on-ramp of a road leading into the desert. There were no people around. I had walked about a mile to get to this place, so I could hitchhike south out of the city. It was an eerie place, especially when it began to get dark. I didn't feel safe, and my fear grew as I watched a dark-skinned man in tattered clothing walk straight toward me.

From about 20 feet away, the man stopped and pulled out a very large knife, almost like a small machete. Just as he began to take another step toward me, I reached into the small of my back and pulled out the six-inch hunting knife that I always carried with me in Africa.

The man stopped again. He stared at me. Although I was petrified, I simply stood still, holding the knife in his direction, and waited.

Many seconds seem to pass. I could tell that the man was trying to decide what to do.

Nothing was said.

Finally, he put the huge knife back inside his clothing, turned around, and walked away.

My heart was racing, but the incident was over. I finally heard my own thoughts, *Please, dear Lord, be with me,* which I was unconsciously repeating in my mind as if a mantra of protection in life and in death. I was 20 years old.

***

My first knife was a small pocket knife my father bought for me at a national park. I cherished it. My uncle gave me a buck knife. My grandpa gave me his Old Timer, a kind of pocket knife. In junior high, I bought a switchblade from a kid at school.

Growing up, we'd bring knives to school and play games where we'd throw them into the ground. If the knife stuck in, the other kid would have to leave one foot planted and with the other, try to step to where the knife was stuck in the ground. If he couldn't make the splits wide enough, he'd lose. We also threw them at cardboard boxes, played Ninjas with our knives, and made wood carvings. Little did I know then that knives would surface multiple times throughout my life.

***

I'd been out at a nightclub with friends near Montmartre, Paris until about 1:30 am. Heading home in different directions, my friends had left.

I was standing alone on the underground platform of the Pigalle Métro Station waiting for a train. There were no other people around until a guy who must have also been in his twenties entered. He began walking toward me. He had a scraggly beard, and he was skinny. He wore loose jeans and an unbuttoned flannel over a T-shirt. He walked right up to me, and within a few feet, he pulled out a small switchblade, clicked it open, and said in French, "Give me your wallet."

I had been actively training Muay Thai kickboxing in Paris, and I had trained other martial arts at the Inosanto Academy back in Los Angeles, much of which dealt with unfortunate situations in which a knife was involved. I felt like I was in great shape. Without even thinking about it, I lifted both of my hands into a boxing stance and said in a matter-of-fact voice, "*Je suis prêt,*" or "I'm ready." I didn't move a muscle, and I stared directly into his brown eyes. Without even considering what he was going to do, my would-be mugger simply put the knife down, turned around, and walked away as casually as he had walked toward me.

After this incident, you'd imagine that I'd have a jolt of adrenaline, but there was nothing. All I thought was how strange it was that someone had just pulled a knife on me, but I felt like it was an exchange as benign as if he had walked up and asked the time. He evidently saw in my eyes that this was one time where pushing the issue wouldn't go well for him, and he decided it wasn't worth it.

***

I was invited to travel from Paris to Normandy to stay with a friend I had met back in the USA, who was living on the coast of France. I didn't have enough money to take a train, so I took the subway as far as I could to get to the roads leading out of the city. Next I found what I'd thought was a good place to get a ride.

I waited hours and hours before, finally, a guy in a diesel Volvo stopped and asked where I was going. I told him, and he said, "Okay, get in."

Once in the car, we began driving, and he started telling me that he was the producer for pornographic films. I didn't think much about it, but then he started asking me questions about the size of my private parts, etc. Really starting to feel awkward, I tried to be as polite as possible when he suggested that I act in one of his films. I hated the whole thing, but I was desperate to continue my trip, knowing that it would be hard to find another ride.

That was when he deviated from the route we had discussed. He turned off the main road.

"What are you doing?" I asked anxiously.

"Oh, this way is faster," he said, but I knew that the direction he was going did not go anywhere near where I wanted to go. I could see that he was sweating. He had both hands at ten o'clock and two o'clock on the top of his brown steering wheel.

"Stop the car!" I shouted.

He didn't stop.

"Stop the car!" I shouted again more intently, and I whipped out my knife from the small of my back. I held the large knife in my right hand with the blade facing downward out of the bottom of my fist in a stabbing position. I shouted, "Do not move your hands, or I will kill you. Pull over right now!"

The guy did not move his hands and had a shocked and frightful look on his face. He began to pull over to the side of the road.

Looking at him intently, I waited for the car to stop. During this, I very clearly envisioned what I would do if he didn't stop the car. I wasn't going to stab him in the chest. I was going to stab this revolting man with all my might right through the back of his right hand.

Even before the car stopped. I had a weird vision of this frustrated pervert trying to jack off with a hole through his hand.

I got out of the car and watched him drive away. I was in a much worse place to get a ride. I was furious, but at least I was safe. Out of thousands of miles of hitchhiking, that was the worst ride I ever had.

***

Popper and I had a name for the things we wanted to bring with us before we went out. "Have you got your emergency kit?" one of us would ask.

"Of course," was always the response.

The kit was a flask, a lighter, and a knife.

In my mid-twenties and early thirties, I spent a lot of time with members of outlaw motorcycle clubs and other intense riders. Knives in this scene were common and about as normal as wearing a watch. I always had one on me, as did most of the guys I was with. Popper was one of these guys.

On one particular night, Popper, Captain, RJ, Tim, and I were sitting out front of the Ramada Inn at tables watching the parade of motorcycles racing up and down the strip. We'd been drinking since about half past noon and were a bit lit up, or at least I was. Earlier in the day, I had my hunting knife on my belt as always, and a cop asked me to put it away, so I stuffed it into the front of my pants.

My riding buddies and I ended up sharing one of the tables with a few members of a support club of one of the big five outlaw clubs. All was going well. One of the guys, who was relatively large, thick, and with a big beard, said to my buddy Popper, "Hey, you look like John Popper."

We all said that we knew that, and that was why we called him Popper. His real name was Dennis, but that didn't stop him from signing autographs for music fans from time to time when they thought he was the real thing.

Then the guy looked at Tim, saying, "And you look like Roger Daltrey."

Sure, not an exact match, but we could kinda see it.

"Ha, ha," the guy then said, looking at me, "and you look like George Michael."

Not really impressed with this claim, I said, "Come on, really?"

At this point I wasn't mad. It was even slightly funny.

Next he leaned over and said to a few people at a neighboring table, "Look, it's George Michael." So, he was making a bigger deal of it, no longer to be funny, but to push buttons.

"All funny, man," I said, "but the joke's over, and I'm going to need you to take it back."

"George Michael, the gay guy at our table," he continued, laughing and pointing at me in a provoking manner.

In other circumstances, I could have ignored this, but we were in an intense crowd, I was wearing a ripped-up, road-proven Levi's jacket and black vest, which should have made him know that I wouldn't stand for being made fun of in a disrespectful way like that.

"One more chance," I said, "or it's on." I was very directly threatening him at this moment, and he knew it.

"George Michael," he again repeated, pointing at my face and laughing.

"Okay," I said.

I pushed my chair back and stood up with my hands wide in a provoking gesture, "Let's go."

This was when I realized exactly how big this thick, bearded man was. He stood up tall, and it was like he kept growing and growing.

Holy shit, I said to myself.

He was an absolute giant, well over six feet tall, and even wider and more solid-looking than I could tell while we were sitting. But I couldn't back down. I had called him out.

We were in a crowd of people, and there were even cops around, but I knew that as good of a fighter as I was, this hulk could crush me. I immediately felt my knife-handle sticking into my gut under the front of my pants belt, so I reached in as if grabbing myself, but pulled my hand out with the large knife. I held it with the blade facing down out of the bottom of my fist. Then I clicked into crazy-person mode.

"I'm going to kill you," I said. "I'm going to cut your balls off," I continued with a wound-up, psychotic face and with my eyes rolling back. "Let's go, let's go, you're dead, you fucking little piss." I was waving and pumping the knife up and down, staring into his face. Saliva was even coming out of my mouth. "Let's go, let's go," I kept repeating viciously as if I were a rabid dog.

At this point the ogre decided that it was totally in his best interest not to push this fight. I knew that he either had a knife or gun himself, but maybe because I had drunk enough Jack Daniel's and beer, I was drunk enough that I didn't care. I didn't even consider backing down.

The guy, coaxed by his two friends, quickly turned and walked away off the patio and into the crowd of people funneling along the packed sidewalk.

I was very lucky, not only lucky that I didn't get sent to the hospital or get killed—I was lucky that I didn't do that to him. What a horribly different life I would have had sitting behind bars for years over a ridiculous comment that I looked like George Michael. While "Stupid things are fun" is my second favorite motto, this was not fun. It was simply stupid.

I think after the incident, I laughed with my friends that I had chased away the huge, threatening beast, but when I woke up sober, but with a headache, the next morning, I realized how lucky I had been. I felt almost sick to my stomach.

***

I was in Colorado Springs with another group of outlaw bikers. We ended up in a standoff with another group. We were face-to-face ready for a bar brawl with about six on our side and ten on theirs. I noticed at least one of the people we were preparing to fight get a blade ready.

We ended up winning the standoff, and afterwards, while I was getting on my bike outside in the parking lot, and the adrenaline rush began to wane, I thought of how close that confrontation came to multiple people ending up in the hospital or worse. In the end, it was an intense and exhilarating night, and it all worked out. And that brings us to my number one, very favorite motto: "Things work out."

I still like knives. I've got hunting knives from Alaska, Maasai blades from Kenya, stilettos from Thailand, and more. I've got favorites for this and that purpose, but mostly knives for me are for utility, for camping, or small pocket knives for cutting tight ribbons off Christmas presents. I have a very strong feeling that my playing with knives is now mostly limited to things that won't get me sent to jail or to the grave. They simply remain souvenirs, maybe even metaphors, of some of the events in my life that I look forward to passing on to my children one day.

Your Turn to Explore

What is the most serious confrontation you've ever been in during your life? What happened and how was it resolved?

Is it better to solve confrontations with physical strength or with words? How could it depend on the circumstances?

Do Something Extraordinary: Think of a time when you really had to overcome an obstacle that made you stronger in the end. Refine this into a story that shows how you persevered and benefited from the experience and share this story with someone.

FIFTEEN

PENCIL FOOT

Los Angeles, USA. 1991. Twenty-Two Years Old

When I got to UCLA, I had the absolute worst dorm room on the entire campus. No kidding, the absolute worst room out of all the dorms. The factors that prove it: the room was in the basement of Dykstra Hall. It had a small window with a view of a dirt berm. It was a rare three-person room. It was on the only all-male floor on campus. That floor was notorious; it was called "The Dungeon." And my room was squished between the loud student laundry room and the smelly trash shoot. All this should confirm that my room was the worst room on the worst floor of all of UCLA.

Being an optimistic person, I resolved myself to the fact that I was in the worst room on campus. Then it got worse. One of the guys across the hall began playing music from the animated Disney film *The Little Mermaid* on volume 11 ... over and over and over. He played the soundtrack from start to finish and again from start to finish. The funny thing was that he was a giant tattooed Samoan guy, but evidently this particular CD helped him study. It certainly didn't make my room any better.

Such is life. I can roll with the punches, and my roommates were pretty cool. One was trying to get into a fraternity, so he was gone a lot, and the other one was from Colorado.

When I was invited to play a pick-up softball game on the UCLA intramural sports field a few days after I arrived, I didn't have any tennis shoes. I asked if I could borrow shoes from my roommate from Colorado. He said yes.

The shoes fit perfectly, and I excitedly walked down Bruin Walk to the field, met quite a few new people, and we began the game. My team easily struck out the other team's first three batters, and it was our turn to bat. I was the third at bat in our unofficial line-up. When I got to the plate, no one had gotten to first base yet. I said to myself that I was going to do it. I was confident about it. I looked at the empty blue and gold gym bag, which acted as first base, and I envisioned hitting the ball and sprinting to it.

When the pitch came, I swung with all my might and, with a ping, connected with the first pitch. As the ball went whizzing by first base into the outfield, I sprinted, hoping to beat the throw to the base. I barely beat the ball when I ran through the base. However, as I planted my foot on the bag, I felt a wildly sharp pain.

"Ouch, ouch, ouch, ouch," I uttered loudly as I slowed down, trying not to plant on my left foot again. When I finally stopped, the other players began gathering around to see what was wrong.

"I think I stepped on a lock, and I broke my foot," I explained, thinking that there was a combination lock attached to the gym bag that I had stepped on as I'd run through the base. I began to feel a bit dizzy. Still trying to process what had happened, I put my hands on my knees and looked down at my foot.

By this point, pretty much everyone was around me.

"Oh my gosh," I said as I looked down at my foot. "Look," I said, pointing down at my shoe. I saw the point-end of a thick black pencil sticking straight up out of the top of the middle of my tennis shoe. The pencil must have been inside the bag, and I'd somehow stepped on it just right. It went in the bottom of the shoe, through my foot, and was sticking out of the top of the shoe.

"Oh, my gosh," many of the people around me said in unison.

Instinctively, I reached down and tried to pull the pencil out, but it didn't budge.

Everyone was grossed out. The girl standing to my right fainted, and I felt a bit queasy from the shock myself. As a few of the people moved their attention to try to help the girl who had passed out, I sat on the grass. Others were still just staring at the odd sight of the pencil through my foot.

I could see the UCLA medical center from where I was. I just wanted a few people to help me hobble the few blocks to the center, but one of the attendants from the rec center insisted that an ambulance come to the field to get me.

In the end, the doctor had to cut the borrowed tennis shoe off my foot. Next, he spent five minutes taking photos of my impaled pencil foot before finally trying to pull the pencil out, but it was too tight, so the doctor had to cut the pencil out. After an X-ray, the doctor said that miraculously, the pencil didn't snap any bones, ligaments, or tendons, and it would just take a bit of time to heal naturally even if it would leave a scar. However, I was forced to begin my first week of classes at UCLA on crutches.

Before the pencil incident, I was excited to begin school and get into a normal routine at UCLA, but it seemed that even in California, I certainly wasn't going to get away with things being normal.

After my first quarter at the school, however, I got to move out of my diabolical dungeon dorm room to the fourth floor of Dykstra with a chosen roommate, Dan Royce. My remaining time in the UCLA dorm was a magical time of studying in the common area, eating in the crammed cafeteria, and having long conversations with Amy, Ray, Ted, Nora, and other friends, either in the hallway or in our rooms, enjoying the sunny views of Westwood.

As soon as my foot was healed, I also rejoined the softball games, but we were sure never to use a gym bag for a base again.

Your Turn to Explore

Do you have a random, strange, or funny experience from when you were younger? What was it?

How do some bad situations actually make life more enjoyable as a whole?

Do Something Extraordinary: To your children or some other young folks in your life, in great detail, tell them about a random, strange, or funny experience you had when you were younger. Also, think of any ways you grew from the incident.

SIXTEEN

BITES, STINGS, AND OTHER DISGUSTING THINGS

USA, Asia, South America, Africa. 1975–1995

I used to think that I could control bugs. Admittedly, I was six years old when I thought that. Let me explain.

Mark and I were having a discussion in the front yard of my mom's parents' house on Meridian Lake. Mark informed me that bees don't sting in the dark. I decided to test it.

It was a nice warm day, and I saw a yellow and black bee buzzing around a dandelion. To test the theory, I cupped my hands around the bee, trying to make sure no light got in from the cracks of my fingers. I stood up smiling and started walking toward my friend. The bee could either see just fine or didn't care that it was dark because it stung me right in the middle of my palm. My failed test would leave me with a painfully sore hand for about three days.

It was that same summer that I was visiting a house on the Puget Sound that belonged to my dad's parents' friends, Rosy and

Irene. Along with my grandma and grandpa, Rosy and Irene were sipping bourbon and water in the grassy yard by the rocky beach when I saw a large garter snake. My grandpa had seen me catch small garter snakes at my house. I loved doing it, so he suggested I catch this one.

I was daunted by the size of this particular snake, which must have been about 2.5 feet long, much bigger than the ten-inch-long snakes I was used to catching, but I was always one to accept a challenge.

Here's what happened: as soon as I picked up the snake, it spun around and clamped onto my hand. Fighting back shock and tears, I got it off me and let it return to the rocks by the water as quickly as I could.

It seems that the lessons of this summer didn't stick because even later in life, I kept getting bit, stung, or worse by the wonderful world of nature.

***

I was 21 and walking through dense trees and thick foliage in Khao Yai, Thailand when it happened. I grabbed a leafy tree trunk to try to gain my balance after jumping to avoid a small cobra that quickly passed almost right under me. And that's how I got bitten—by a poisonous spider. I could see the two dots of the bite right away.

It took about three hours before my hand had swollen to the size of an orange with puss oozing out of the area of the bite between my thumb and index finger. As I was in a remote area, I couldn't get to any hospital. Much to my relief the swelling went down at about the same rate that it had grown.

Also, on this Thailand excursion, I was hiking with a guy from Germany. We spent about eight hours silently creeping around the jungle, hoping for a glimpse of monkeys, deer, elephants, or other majestic animals in the area.

What we did see—hundreds of leeches inching toward us on the wet brown leaves that coated the jungle floor. Already warned about the leeches, we'd tucked our pant bottoms into our socks. About the leeches dropping on us from the trees above, we even avoided those. Indeed, we were prepared and skilled jungle trekkers.

Well, that wasn't the case. Although we'd thought we had outsmarted them, by the end of the hike, we discovered that the leeches had made their way through the knitting of our socks. Our feet and ankles were covered with large leeches now fat with our own blood.

***

It was in South America along the Maroni River where I had a run-in with two other nasty creatures. One incident involved a swarm of piranhas that managed to rip about ten very small chunks from my ankles and feet after I'd fallen over some boulders into the river. The other was a sting, on the tip of my right elbow, by a small rust-colored scorpion. That sting rendered the right half of my body paralyzed for three days.

***

Bites, stings, and poison are one thing, but it is sometimes the things we can't initially see where things start to get really gross. While crossing a section of the Moroccan desert in North Africa, I was foolishly convinced to drink a bit of un-boiled well water. I paid for it. I contracted cholera, which left me with two days of severe vomiting, diarrhea, and dehydration. I was alone walking through the desert during this, and I was literally saved by two guys who happened to be traveling along the same remote path on motorcycles and who took me to the nearest town to get help.

As I traveled through Asia, Africa, and South America, I was generally very exposed to the elements. I was not staying at fancy, clean hotels, but rather in people's houses, huts, or very commonly out in the open, either in a tent or under the trees or stars. I was also eating whatever food I could get and often washing only in rivers and streams. With this extended exposure, I ended up contracting some gnarly diseases including staphylococcus or staph infection, leishmaniasis, and the dreaded bot flies. I contracted both leishmaniasis and bot flies on the banks of rivers in South America, and as a gauge on how nasty they are, they are both listed in the top ten most disgusting parasites for humans to get.

About the bot flies—they started as tiny eggs injected into my left leg behind the knee. These microscopic organisms, however, are on a mission to grow, and now surrounded by my flesh, growth was as simple as eating as much of the meat of my leg as possible. The traditional method of extracting them is to place animal meat over the holes that develop on the host's skin. As the parasites begin to suffocate, they actually eat their way into the animal meat placed over the skin as a way to escape. Remove the meat, and *voila*, the bot flies are out.

In my case, I didn't know I had them until I returned to the United States. Two large holes developed, and a line of puss and blood continuously ran down the back of my leg. It wasn't until I saw the tropical disease specialist at the University of Virginia that I learned I had bot flies. Laughably, I think the doctor was excited to be able to treat the disease since he had never seen an actual case of the flies before.

Other ailments that I contracted during my travels aren't as visually disgusting as bot flies; however, malaria is certainly the greatest killer of all of them. I attribute my first occurrence of malaria due to a Nigerian policeman stealing my tent as a bribe. After this happened, I spent many, many nights sleeping out in the African wilderness without any protection from the dreaded mosquitoes.

I first began feeling sick in Central African Republic. I had plans to travel up to Egypt, but I cut things short based on how ill I felt. I flew to London where I rested in the squatted flat of some young punk rockers I had met. Then I flew back to the USA on the first available flight I could afford.

As soon as I got home, I visited our local neighborhood doctor. He couldn't figure out what was wrong with me other than acute fever. I saw him two times in a span of three days. During those three days, I was wrought in pain, shaking chills, and my nights were wide-awake hallucinatory nightmares during which I sometimes seriously considered that death would be a great option. When I returned to Dr. Rutherford after three days with my fever not getting better, he ran more tests.

I'll never forget the look on Dr. Rutherford's face after he had checked my blood under the microscope for the second time.

"Erik," he said, "sit down."

I thought this was funny since I was already sitting at the edge of the examination table.

He continued with a worried look, "There is something eating away at your blood cells at a very rapid rate, and if we can't figure out what it is ..." He didn't say the last words. He simply put his palms up and raised his shoulders with a perplexed look that said, "Who knows what will happen?" which I interpreted as, "You are gonna die."

This was, in fact, what he meant. Immediately, he put a call in to a hematologist, and he sent me there right away.

The hematologist was expecting me. Knowing I had been to Africa, I think he already knew what the problem was. Although the waiting room was packed, I was rushed to a back room where he drew blood. Within 12 minutes of arriving, he returned to me with my mother sitting next to me.

He said, "Good news—you have malaria." It was obvious that he liked his ironic statement that having malaria was good news, but at least he knew how to treat the falciparum malaria I had.

He immediately gave me some quinine tablets, and almost instantly I felt better. I remained sitting limply in the chair, but I could tell that the doctor felt I was out of danger as soon as I'd ingested the medicine. He still wanted my mom and me to wait for a few hours, just to be sure.

While sitting with us before we were ready to leave, he said in a still bit of a nervous voice, "When you arrived here, based on the level of red and white blood cells left in your blood and the acceleration of fever in your body, in my opinion, you only had hours to live."

My second stint with malaria was six years later and occurred while spending three months of anthropological research with the Wayana Indians in South America. I was faithfully taking Mefloquine as a prophylaxis but sleeping for nearly 90 days in a hammock outside was enough to break through the protection. Ultimately, when I got back to the USA, I was told that I was the first case the doctors knew of for someone to have contracted vivax malaria while faithfully taking Mefloquine.

**

Four times that I didn't get stung or bitten, but which are honorable mentions due to their being very close calls include (1) the time I woke up in a Thailand guest house with a large black, yellow, and red centipede cuddled up against me in bed; (2) the time in South America that I woke up with a furry tarantula on my face; (3) the time I almost sat on a crocodile in the Amazon while attempting to take a dump along a river bank; and (4) the time in Africa which really could have been the worst bite of my life. For this one, I am sharing the story.

I was walking in a remote area of savannah as I often did, and I was just setting up my camp. I'd lit my fire when I heard the sound of a motorcycle getting louder and louder. Since I was alone with nothing around, I became frightened that it might be someone approaching to steal my gear. It ended up being a Cameroonian police officer.

"What are you doing?" the officer asked, as he turned the motorcycle off. The old motorcycle began ticking as it cooled down, and a long shadow from the officer and his motorcycle made a dark streak through the sunlit yellow and orange grassy area I had selected for the night.

"Just camping here for the night," I responded. I thought it was a perfect spot.

"There are *A LOT* of lions around here," he informed me with emphasis and a tone of annoyance. He seemed dumbfounded that I'd even think about sleeping exposed in the bush, especially without a tent.

"It's okay," I said, "I've been sleeping in the bush most of the time for weeks now."

"Not here," he continued. "This is one of the most populated areas for lions, and there are extremely aggressive lions all over this place."

Since I had camped a lot through Africa, I still would have been comfortable staying, but the officer insisted that I pack up my things and get on the motorcycle with him. It was only minutes until we arrived at a remote police station that also seemed to double as a ranger station for a nearby game reserve. The police-man collected my passport, so I couldn't leave, and he said that I had to sleep on the front porch of the station.

It was just dark when I slipped into my sleeping bag on the hard cement porch. I was annoyed that I had to stay because I had hoped to get a very early start the next day, and now I'd have to wait for my passport until later the following morning.

Just as I mumbled, "Shoot," to myself, I heard the first roar of a giant cat. My chest vibrated, and I jumped up in a panic. It felt like it was right on me. I had heard roaring lions many times while sleeping out in the bush, but from much farther away.

I was suddenly very happy that I was under the awning of the covered porch. I was even more happy when a half hour later, I could see the silhouettes of a few male and female lions circling the edges of the compound. As they roared through the night, I was comforted by the safety of the porch. At this point, I was, indeed, ecstatic that the officer had noticed me out in the bush and had forced me to move camp.

Certainly, the incident with the lions in Cameroon is one of the many times when it seemed that someone was looking out for me. I thanked the officer in my head, and I thanked God as well. Some of my friends who have heard all the stories of my life say that I'm either the luckiest person in the world because I always seem to circumvent demise, or the unluckiest because I've had so many horrible things happen to me. I like to think that with a little help from the saviors such as the guys on the motorcycle who rescued me in Morocco, the Wayana who took care of me in the Amazon, the doctors who treated me in the USA, and even the annoyed police officer in Cameroon, things always worked out. Yes, my favorite motto: "Things work out."

I would love to have avoided the scorpion, cholera, bot flies, and malaria, but if asked, I would not trade my experiences for the safety of never being in danger in the first place.

Your Turn to Explore

Have you ever been in a situation where you took a risk to accomplish something you wanted to do? What was it, and was it worth it?

At what point does the risk of doing something outweigh the potential benefit?

Do Something Extraordinary: Think of something that you want to do, but you're a bit scared of doing. Picture yourself as ten or 20 years older than you are now and ask your future self if you'd regret NOT doing it. And, if at all reasonable, do it.

SEVENTEEN

IT COULD'VE BEEN ME

California, USA. 1997–2007

We were riding up in the Santa Monica Mountains above Malibu. We had already been by the Rock Store and had just stopped at one of the overlooks to take a quick break and look out over stunning hills lined with winding roads. It was a beautiful, sunny day.

As the group began pulling out, I was feeling great and decided to rip off a burnout. I pulled in the clutch, and with the precise timing I had built up with a lot of practice, I dropped the clutch and twisted my wrist, pulling the throttle down. The rear wheel might have been spinning, but this time it was much more than just a burnout. The front wheel of my bike slowly pulled up into the air. I kept steadily rolling on the throttle, and as I shifted into second gear with the wheel still in the air, the front of the bike returned to the ground as gracefully as it had come up.

I loved it, but my wife on the back was furious. It was her extra weight over the rear wheel that turned my planned burnout into a wheelie—my first ever wheelie! She pounded my helmet with an open hand a few times, yelling, "Don't do that again! You about gave me whiplash!"

I was too excited to care that she was mad, but I said okay with a giant smile on my face. I certainly didn't want to tell her that it was an accident. I was even more proud of my bike than ever.

The motorcycle was a 2000 Night Train, but once I was done customizing it, even the most veteran biker wouldn't be able to tell you what kind of bike she was without looking at the VIN. I first received the motorcycle as a signing bonus for beginning to work for Glenn Bartels at his motorcycle rental shop in Marina Del Rey. When I was given the bike, she already had a stage two kit, a hefty 211 cam, and a powerful black Thunder-Header exhaust system. Even before I did more work to the Monster, she had more power and engine displacement than a Volkswagen Beetle.

It wasn't 20 minutes after taking ownership of the bike that Glenn walked back to the service area and saw me taking a hacksaw to the license plate bracket and rear fender. In the end, we cut the frame, raking her out to 42 degrees. We put on ape-hanger handlebars and four-inch-over fork tubes. A friend made a custom seat, and we painted her black with red gunsights on the side of the tank. We switched out all the externals like the rocker box and primary covers and oil tank with a friend's Fatboy, so he had a black Fatboy, and I had a chrome Night Train.

The *piece de résistance* was the sissy bar, which was the end of a sawed off double-barrel shotgun. The horn, blinkers, front fender, air filter cover, and anything else that didn't make her go faster went into the trash can. She was also as finely tuned as you could get. Cody, one of Glenn's mechanics, was a master, and I told him that if he kept the Monster right, he could ride her anytime he wanted. It was a successful relationship.

I'm not entirely sure if it is correct or not, but I often used to say that the Monster was one of the fastest street-legal Harley-Davidsons in Los Angeles. Cody seemed to agree. We'd already done after-market ignition, thicker voltage wires, a robust racing clutch basket, but there was one more thing we wanted to do. Finally, Cody put on a Mikuni 42 flat-side carburetor with an exposed K&N air filter.

It was Wednesday, which meant bike night, and I couldn't wait to ride. I rode every day because I didn't own a car but riding with our crew during bike night was always special.

As we got off work at about six, we began on the Westside this time. Since the guys from our group lived on both the Westside and the Valley, our routine was usually to stop at a bar either in West Los Angeles or the San Fernando Valley, ride to the opposite side for a second bar or tavern stop, and then end in Hollywood, so we were at the top of the hill between the two. This made sense because it was as much about the riding as the stops in-between. We'd speed along freeways or city streets, zipping through the lights and sounds of the city in a parade of motor-powered chariots. Usually at about one or two in the morning, we'd split up from Hollywood and go our various directions home.

We were a very aggressive group. We'd often be over eight bikes strong riding 60 or more miles per hour up Melrose or Santa Monica Boulevard, and often over a 100, cutting lanes on the 405 or 101 Freeways.

One night, we were getting close to our last stop of the evening, and we were riding with Betty, a great rider. She was even on the Discovery Channel program *Chicks Who Ride*. For some reason, everyone was riding a bit more slowly than normal, so I decided to change that. We were at a red light on Cahuenga and Hollywood Boulevards, and I decided to spice things up with a burnout. After all, I wanted to impress Betty.

When the light turned green, Betty was right next to me in the same lane. I dropped the clutch and spun the throttle as I'd done many times, but it didn't go as before. Because of my new carburetor, there was so much more power to my rear wheel than I was used to, it slid wildly to the right, then to the left, and then totally out of control. As the rear tire heated up, the front wheel came off the ground and the rear end of the bike spun past the front. It happened so fast that I don't remember exactly what happened, but I do remember spinning on the ground across Hollywood Boulevard with a crowd of people from the street corner watching.

Other than a bit of blood on my knees, I was fine, and you can imagine how quickly I wanted to get out of there before the cops arrived. As I picked up my bike in the middle of the road, one ape-hanger handlebar was facing straight up, but the left handlebar was angled down at about a 45-degree angle. I still can't believe how I didn't get hurt worse sliding along the middle of the intersection along with my burning-hot motorcycle engine and spinning chain and wheels, but I didn't.

The reset computer on my bike would take one minute before she would start again, and that 60 seconds felt like forever. At 61 seconds, I fired up the bike and rode away as quickly as possible with my right hand up in the air, and my left way down by my knee, as I was shifting with my thumb. We ended up quickly getting to the next bar, and we laughed it off with a shot of Jack Daniel's and a Budweiser.

Jack and Bud were generally the drinks of choice for most of us, and it was exciting to pull up to a bar with eight to 20 motorcycles and take the place over. We'd roll up in a deafening rumble of customized bikes, and some places would already have spots right out front blocked off for us. Other times, we had to fend for ourselves.

I think our most unique parking job was one night when one of the guys in our group got a job working at The Standard Hotel on Sunset Boulevard. The Standard is an extremely upscale joint with a great rooftop bar and a strict dress code. It is for this reason that we all wanted to go mess with Andy.

It was his first night as security, and we rode up in our thunderous cloud of noise, as always. Since there wasn't anywhere to park, we just took over the entire entrance, parking on the sidewalk and in the valet zone between the Porsches and Aston Martins. When no room was left, quite a few of us rode right up into the flowerbeds and parked between the bushes. We all thought it was hilarious, but not Andy. We let all the freaked-out, panicking employees of The Standard know that it was okay because we knew the security guard. It is a wonder that he didn't get fired.

Andy was a hulk of a man. He had short blond hair and Arnold Schwarzenegger-type muscles that bulged. I think his biceps were probably as large as my neck. He was a super nice guy, and he'd only been to jail one time for beating up a parking meter ticket guy. Andy should have gotten a medal rather than get arrested for that one, but such is the justice system.

Andy had a very hopped-up, high-compression Harley-Davidson FXR. When Cody and I got my bike, lovingly referred to as "The Monster" or alternatively as "The Beast," in as good of shape as possible, the sound alone let people know that she was an iron race horse. Andy and I knew that it was going to come to a contest at one point, and it finally did.

It was about one thirty in the morning near the end of one of our Wednesday bike rides. We'd already been to one tavern and two bars, and we were speeding home wildly. Just at the very top of Sherman Pass going from Sherman Oaks toward Westwood, Andy decided—it was on. We were already going about 90 when he pulled up next to me, deliberately looked me in the eye, and dramatically twisted his throttle.

The start of the race was as evident as if there had been a green flag waving in front of us. I spun my wrist all the way over, feeling the throttle stop at its farthest rotation in the direction of speed. I very slowly began passing Andy. We were continuing down the steep grade of the pass, and my speedometer was pegged at 120 miles per hour, but we'd been accelerating long beyond that. My ape-hangers made my body like a parachute, so I had to fight as hard as I could with my stomach muscles to stay forward to the bike. My forward foot controls didn't help either, and at one point, my left foot flew off the side of the peg because of the force of the wind, and my bike dove left. Leaning with all my might, I barely straightened the bike out before plowing into the cement center divider of the freeway.

The noise of my tires running over the loose gravel and debris, left of the carpool lane, was alarming. I could barely breathe with the force of the wind in my face, but I continued to pull on the throttle. I was still in front of Andy, and with my tearing eyes and tunnel vision, I had no idea how far ahead of him I was. Then I was aware of flashing lights in my single rearview mirror.

What? I said in my head in disbelief that any cops could have caught up to us at that speed.

We were near the bottom of the five-mile hill and entering Westwood. I rolled off the throttle and coasted over a quick mile before entering back into the speed of the rest of the world. My heart was still beating, and I finally looked back to see Andy rolling up next to me. However, I did not see any police with flashing lights.

As Andy got to my side, we were only going about 70 miles per hour, which felt very slow. His eyes were huge, ghostly wide, and he simply placed his left hand on my shoulder and held it there for a moment as if thankful for our friendship. Andy wasn't right though, so as he took his hand off my shoulder, I motioned that we should pull off the next exit.

We exited onto Olympic Boulevard, found a parking lot, and got off our bikes. I was shaking because of the adrenaline of my ride, but Andy was even worse. When Navy, who was behind us, pulled in, I learned what had happened. Andy's FXR had a low-profile front fender, and most Harley-Davidson tires are rated for 120 miles per hour. As Andy and I sped along down that hill at about 140 or 150, his tire expanded because of the centripetal force, rubbed his fender, and put him in a high-speed wobble. It was the slapping back and forth of Andy's headlight that had been flashing in my rearview mirror.

Navy, who was behind us on a Road King, said that he wasn't trying to figure out how to avoid Andy and the bike *if* he went down. Instead, Navy was calculating how he could try to miss running over his friend *when* he went down. He was certain that a high-speed accident was to happen. Andy talked about how his bars were flapping back and forth in a "tank slapper" motion. If Andy weren't so strong and coordinated, he'd have been done. The vibration from the force of the wobble was so extreme that both side panels of Andy's FXR had popped off.

Andy calmed down in his aggressive riding for about a week, but then we were right back at it. The adrenaline was addicting, and we felt young and bulletproof. We were great riders, and testing our limits put us in an amazing place.

My pinnacle moment while riding a motorcycle also took place on a Wednesday night. We had a group of about 15 of us. We had met at Johnny Rockets on Melrose and then ended up at Jumbo's Clown Room, which was a comedy strip club in Hollywood where, on some nights, the more hideous the woman dancing, the funnier it was. There was only one strip pole, and it was really much more about the drinking than the stripping that made this place fun.

We'd been there for a while when the call came in. "Red's bike is down," R-Jay said as we gathered around.

This wasn't rare. The more customized a bike, the more is going to happen with it, and on this night, the exhaust pipe on Red's radical Sportster fell off while he was riding to meet us. Everyone slapped money on the bar and started funneling out. Just to make sure we had left enough, I quickly waved the barmaid over and asked what we owed. She didn't even check but said about 150 bucks. My wife counted all the cash our group had thrown on the bar, and she stopped counting when we saw that it was way more than enough. We threw in 20 more and headed out.

Once my wife and I got to my bike, we were at the far end of the long parking lot over 100 feet from the other riders who were with us. They were lined up in a pack turning right out of the parking lot. I started the Beast and positioned her straight toward our group, which was far in front of us. There was a long line of about 100 people waiting to get into a club next door to Jumbo's. I said, "Hold on."

At this point, my wife knew that when I said, "Hold on," it was much more than passively putting her hands around my sides, so she hugged my stomach tightly, anticipating what was going to come, and she buried the side of her helmet into my back.

I let the Monster rip!!!!!! I dropped the clutch and really pulled the throttle with conviction. There was no halfway. And I knew that with weight over the back wheel, it was not going to be a burnout. Even with a raked-out bike and extended front end, the front wheel shot toward the heavens. It came up so high that my arms felt like they were behind my head holding onto the 18-inch-high handlebars. My face seemed inches from my gas tank, and I held it all the way through first gear. People in the line were cheering before the front end of the bike was back down, and I loved it knowing that this stunt would never be repeated so flawlessly.

After riding together almost every Wednesday, a longer ride out of L.A. about once a month, and some multi-day rides to bike events, our aggressiveness continued to mount. We had our routines and places to visit. One of them was Blacky's owned by a guy named Stan on Lankershim Boulevard. It wasn't a biker bar, but it was an edgy place, and Stan was a biker. He had an old Panhead, and he loved us.

Often it would be crowded with people jockeying around the bar trying to order drinks, but as the sound of our bikes approached, Stan's bartenders would stop everything and start pouring shots of Jack Daniel's and setting bottles of Budweiser on the bar. When we walked in, taking off our jackets, we'd saunter over to the bar, squeeze through the crowd, and pick up our ready-made drinks with a cheer and a tip of the bottle toward the bartenders.

Although we were having a blast, I started to realize how often we were on the edge. It was no longer occasional but becoming almost every time we rode. One evening, over my fourth or fifth beer, I said, "You guys, you know that if we keep riding like this, either we're all going to go to jail for a very long time, or someone is going to die." Everyone agreed, but it didn't stop.

About a month later, there was a ride that I happened not to be on. I was told that it was just like all the other crazy times that we loved. Near the end of the ride, speeding up the 405 at about 90 miles per hour, splitting lanes, and loving the thrill, a car slammed on its breaks in front of the group, and two of our bikes went for the same gap between the cars. It was the slight rubbing of one rear wheel with the front wheel of another. At 90 miles per hour, this was all it took, and both bikes, two riders, and two girlfriends went down in a tangle of bikes, cars, and concrete. It was Marty who died.

When I heard the news, I was shocked at the reality of what had happened, but I really wasn't surprised. It was bound to happen. That incident made all of us realize that we weren't invincible after all. We had all become addicted to the thrill of the edge, but the problem was, we kept pushing the limits. As Hunter S. Thompson wrote in his book *Hells Angels*, "The Edge ... there is no honest way to explain it because the only people who really know where it is are the ones who have gone over." Marty found it, but he's not here to tell us about it, and we can't have him back.

As I think of the loss of this great human being, I also think of the times I pushed riding beyond the point of excitement and well into the region of ludicrous. I think of the time I raced a sport bike in heavy traffic from Palm Springs to Los Angeles. It wasn't about whose bike was faster as much as about who was willing to take the most risks between cars. I think about the time I woke up with such a headache after a biker party that I started off the day with a few shots to "clear my head" before the long ride home, and I was indifferently drinking whiskey out of a flask in front of all the spectators at a station while pumping gas. Afterwards, I continued to ride at over 100 miles per hour carelessly weaving in and out of traffic. I think about splitting lanes between semis and buses with inches on each side of my handlebars. I think about racing up near LAX airport and sliding by a friend in a rear wheel skid at about 60 miles per hour just to be funny. Many times, I should have gone down and didn't. I thank God that somehow whether it was skill, luck, or both, I made it through so many precarious situations. In a nostalgic way, I look back fondly on some of our crazy times, but in the end, when I reflect on Marty, I can't help but think, *It could've been me.*

Your Turn to Explore

Have you ever done things that, looking back, were extremely irresponsible?

What causes people to do things that might put their life on the line?

Do Something Extraordinary: Think of one critical time in your life that was exhilarating, happy, fun, frightening, challenging, or somehow amazing. Write a first-person narrative about the experience. Simply tell your story on paper and see what thoughts are generated during your writing.

EIGHTEEN

REFLECTIONS ON GROWTH

In the preceding living-on-the-edge narratives, I didn't always act with good judgment. Reflecting on some of the experiences—my wonderful time in Japan, my days diligently reading books, and joyfully playing with friends at UCLA—are positive moments from my life. But the time in Thailand when I became dangerously close to drug addiction, the numerous nights I spent riding my motorcycle way too fast, and the times I could have been killed in (avoidable) fighting situations or by being exposed to serious illnesses are just as valuable in creating who I am. All these experiences have shaped not only the snapshot of who I am today, but they shape my goals and my vision of the person I want to become tomorrow.

Growth is an amazing thing. It can be one of the greatest rewards as well as greatest motivators. When we look at life, we can recognize that it is not static but a constant movement through space and time. As belonging, purpose, transcendence, and storytelling act as the four pillars of meaning at any given moment, growth acts as a way for us to continually evaluate our experiences, providing both perspective and direction. Perspective, of course, is viewing an issue from different angles, or different places, and that is where the edge comes in. The edge exists beyond the familiar, acting as rocket fuel for growth by quickly enabling us to see our lives from a wider perspective.

As shown by Holocaust survivor and author Viktor Frankl, meaning is created in our lives by our ability to see our future self in some valuable role helping others. Growth, like love, can exist beyond ourselves when we share our experience in aim of benefiting others. The beauty of growth is that we are never a slave to our current condition. Life doesn't move in a straight line, and whether we're moving toward greatness or sliding in a harmful direction, we always possess the basic freedom of choosing our next steps in life and even choosing how we perceive our current state. As Abraham Lincoln famously put it, "Most folks are about as happy as they make up their minds to be." So, make up your mind today and choose to embrace happiness and success in your life.

Your Turn to Explore

What are some areas in your life in which you'd like to grow more?

What are moments from your life that have contributed to you growing in positive or negative directions? Think about how these moments have created who you are today.

Do Something Extraordinary: Growing is often most easily done with the help of other people. Think of someone whom you could ask to help keep you accountable for continuing to grow toward goals you have in your life. If you really want to take this seriously, hire an accountability coach who can quickly help you reach your goals.

YOUR FREE GIFT

Believe it or not, keeping up a steady flow of personal growth is not as simple as it sounds. With our busy lives of work, children, and activities, it is easy to neglect yourself. Don't let this happen. I've created a free interactive calendar filled with suggestions on what you can do to keep a manageable schedule of growth every week. It is also a personal accountability schedule to help you track progress toward your goals. To get this wonderful growth, goal setting, and accountability tool, simply email me with GROWTH & GOALS TOOL in the subject line. Email Erik@ErikSeversen.com or go to www. ErikSeversen.com.

NINETEEN

HAPPINESS AND SUCCESS

Would you rather win 100 million dollars in the lottery or be involved in a horrific traffic accident that leaves you paralyzed from the chest down? Are you sure? If you're like most people, you'd choose the lottery. However, if you're like the people who have actually won 100-million-dollar mega-lotteries or have been paralyzed from an accident, statistically speaking, you'd wish for paraplegia. Studies have shown that the accident survivors are happier with day-to-day simple pleasures than lottery winners.

One of the studies I'm referring to is Philip Brickman, Dan Coates, and Ronnie Janoff-Bulman's 1978 study out of the University of Massachusetts Amherst titled, "Lottery Winners and Accident Victims: Is Happiness Relative?" Their study of 22 lottery winners and 29 paralyzed accident victims found that, contrary to expectation, accident survivors listed more happiness in every-day activities than did the lottery winners. Furthermore, when asked about feelings regarding their future happiness, the permanently paralyzed survivors' average responses scored higher on a scale from totally unhappy (0) to totally happy (5) than those of the lottery winners.

This study from the late 1970s is even less shocking than many of the later stories of people who have won mega-lotteries of hundreds of millions of dollars. With these individuals, many experienced negatively life-changing phenomena, which led to isolation and despair.

Why? Because happiness isn't an end point or a goal to be reached and captured. Rather, happiness is a process, and part of the process is growth. For the paralyzed accident survivor, losing the use of their legs provides them with a goal and a future of hard work to get there. The goal might first be to get better and then to learn to live under totally unfamiliar circumstances. They face a massive challenge to overcome, and most get to it right away with a determination matching that of Olympic athletes.

The mega-lottery winners, on the other hand, are given anything they desire. Want a Beverly Hills mansion? No problem. Want a Lamborghini? Why not get a custom paint job too? Freedom? You'll never have to work another day in your life. Take a trip around the world? You can do it ten times, first-class all the way. Champagne, bourbon? Only top shelf. As much as you want of it. After all, you don't have to get up to go to work tomorrow.

So why, after a year, are the lottery winners often steeped in depression, suicidal thoughts, or on the verge of an alcoholic or drug-addicted tailspin? The answer is that the lottery winners suddenly have everything they want, and there is nothing more to strive towards. We all like to think we'd change the world in a positive way by starting some world-saving charity, but the fact is that mega-lottery winners don't do this. Their purpose, instead, becomes satisfying self-centered wishes, which provide no purpose, no goals, no challenges to overcome. Rarely does anything good come from this situation.

The study of lottery winners and accident victims acts as a clear example highlighting how important it is for us to continue growing throughout our lives. We will never learn everything, and we will never capture happiness or success in a box to keep. Happiness and success are flowing entities that we must recognize as we move through our lives from health to sickness, poverty to wealth, or any other positive or negative change.

The relationship between happiness and success is also not static. Success doesn't cause happiness, and happiness doesn't cause success. Rather, every moment, we live as either a successful and happy person, or we do not. And, the choice isn't made from some external force, but from within each of us.

One successful person might be just starting their journey with loads of debt and an idea, and another successful person might have a thriving multimillion-dollar business. Both individuals may or may not be happy, but each has an equal opportunity to recognize happiness in their life no matter the circumstances. Whether living in a penthouse in San Francisco or a prison cell in San Quentin, we can choose our state of mind. Just like Camus' Sisyphus chose to find meaning in pushing the rock that he was to move up a hill for eternity, we can choose to live with happiness in our lives no matter the circumstances. You see, happiness isn't the goal, but it can actually be the way itself if we chose to live our lives with an intentional desire to love, learn, and contribute.

It is important to note that your life doesn't have to be perfect to love, learn, and contribute. As you've seen in the narratives in this book, I did love, I did strive to learn, and I tried to benefit others, but there were many times I simply made bad decisions. However, I always tried to learn from my experiences and to grow into a better person. I continue to do this every single day.

I pray that as you finish this book highlighting a few moments from my life, you'll work toward your dreams in the space beyond extraordinary while recognizing happiness is a backpack you can pick up and take with you wherever you go, and success is a path of bricks you can follow along your journey. The choice is easy, and the choice is yours, so let's pick up our backpacks and walk along the path of success together, encouraging others as we love and as we grow. Let's follow the path to where growth is easiest, to where learning is paramount, and helping others is standard. Let us take the path out of the comfortable center and adventure toward the edge, that wonderful place beyond extraordinary.

TWENTY

WHAT COMES NEXT?

Southern Russia. 2019. Fifty Years Old

What was I looking for at the top of the mountain?

If I discover the end of a rainbow, I might find a pot of leprechaun's gold. If I locate the X on a pirate's map, I expect to find a buried chest of treasure. But what was I seeking at the summit of Mt. Elbrus, the 18,510-foot peak in southern Russia?

Sure, I might see the overwhelming views of the rugged Caucasus Mountains of Russia and Georgia. And, sure, I might bond in friendship with Chris, my climbing partner. But what exactly was I expecting to find at the top of the mountain other than thin air and an icy summit housing a small plaque marking the highest point in Europe? You see, there was nothing tangible, nothing to "find" there. Or was there?

Reaching the summit was the goal of the climb, but it was the journey rather than the destination where the discovery existed. Would my legs be strong enough to carry me and my heavy pack up the steep glacier? Would my lungs be powerful enough to push through the thin air and exhaustion? Would my skin be thick enough to endure the inclement weather of -30 degrees Fahrenheit and sixty-mile per hour winds? Would fear of unknown crevasses and steep inclines stop me?

You see, the discovery really wasn't on the mountain at all; rather the real discovery on the climb was inside of myself. Upon reaching the summit, yes, we celebrated the success of reaching the highest point we could arrive at, but the real success was knowing that my mind was able to push my body far from anything resembling comfort. I was able to see exactly how hard I could push myself in working toward the goal. And this is exactly like life.

You don't have to climb a mountain to receive the rewarding gift of self-exploration, however. You can do this on a strenuous bicycle ride, run, or other physical exercise. You can do this in business or by examining an esoteric book, or poem, or relationship. Exploration isn't limited to what is outside of ourselves. It may be our interaction with external things—mountains and ideas and people—but the heart of exploration is discovering internally. No matter our circumstances, good or bad, as long as we're conscious, we are capable of choosing to pick up our backpack of happiness and walk along the trail of success. As we traverse our lives, let's choose to explore.

ACKNOWLEDGMENTS

First, I want to thank God without whom I could not have experienced any of the moments that compose my life. Not only is God my creator, God has continually proven to watch over me. He is also a forgiving God who accepts me with all my faults and mistakes included. There are many times I've thought about God while calculating risk during a decision to travel to an unfamiliar, remote area or deciding whether to climb a mountain with hidden crevasses or nearly vertical sections of ice. I have never taken death lightly, and I do not take unnecessary risks, but because I believe that there is a great life waiting for me after death, I'm not afraid to die. The liberation I get by knowing that my death will lead to a wonderful new beginning is one of the reasons I've been comfortable living on the edge in the first place.

Second, I want to thank my wife, Diep. From the day she sat down next to me on a university bus in Virginia, she has been a bright spot in my life. She's also been an amazing support who has stuck with me through wonderful and difficult times. She is the love of my life. My two teenage boys, Jack and Ben, are also an amazing inspiration to me. They remind me that being a person isn't enough. Rather, it is important to be a good person.

Third, my parents and siblings. Life growing up was not perfect, but there was love in my family, and I truly believe that my father's example of hard work, my mother's exposure to Zig Ziglar's motivational business recordings, and my older brother and sister's example of dedication in school and sports was an inspiration to me. This also includes Keith, my amazing foster brother who lived with us for parts of high school.

Fourth, are extraordinary teachers. I've had some horrible teachers growing up, including my wasted kindergarten year where I learned how to punch kids who spit on me but that was about it. My high school counselor, who said I'd never get into UCLA, and others could have derailed my desires to chase dreams, but I choose not to focus on them. Rather, I celebrate the amazing teachers I did have, starting with Mrs. McIntyre at Elmhurst Elementary School in the third and sixth grades, Mr. Druggie in the fourth grade, and Ben Erickson, Mr. Sawyer, and Mrs. T at Washington High School, who each contributed to my evolution from a poor to engaged and inspired student. From UCLA, I want to thank Dr. Peter B. Hammond, who was my mentor and who was the first one to help me believe in my academic potential.

Since, like many things I do in my life, this acknowledgments segment is not your typical blurb, I'm going to continue with a few other amazing people in my life. I want to thank an amazing family whom I don't think I ever thanked. Gordy and Mary Hansen who were my best friend Mike's parents. Gordy was the vice principal at my school at the time he learned I was living in my van, and I was invited to live with the Hansen family for one semester during high school. It was a time I learned what a beautiful, healthy family looked like, and they made me feel part of it.

Next, I want to thank my close group of high school friends whom I continue to love more than 30 years after we graduated together. Kirk, Shawn, Carl, Greg, Jack, Glen, Dave, and Kevin enrich my life daily through their child-like banter on our group text threads. Other close friends from high school include Mary Jane, Dan, James, Lew, and many more. Other friends from my time at Green River College include Gladys, Neil, William, Willy,

Sung, Kathy, Tang, Cecilia, and many others. At UCLA, there was Audrey, Don, Nancy, Faiz, Ken, Roy, Maymuna, Minh, Paul De, and Many others. Notable students who became close friends are Taka, Aun, Juju, Naoki, and many more. There is Sofiane, Sylvie, Susanne, Sandrine, William, Julie and the entire Gallais family in France, the Tallandier family in French Guiana, and Rick and Edy from graduate school at UVA, and my closest riding buddies Wil, C-Ray, Thomas, Ron, Popper, David, Kimo, Ray, and Chad. There are my fellow university teacher colleagues including Jennifer, Kyle, Richard, Bella, Michael, Tara, Judy, Adam, Luba, and many more. In business there is Glenn, Arif, Barry, Jeff, and Chris. I could go on and on, but the main thing I want to say to each of those listed above is that I cherish the time I got to spend with you, and I learned from all of you.

With enthusiasm, I want to thank Nancy Pile, my editor, who always makes my writing better, and I want to thank all the positive people surrounding me in my current projects. From Tony Robbins, Brendon Burchard, Tim Ferriss, David Ramsey, Noa Schecter, Claudia Scheffler, and David Brownlee. Some of you I know only through your seminars, your courses, or your writing, and others I speak with daily. I'm happy that I've learned something from you that has contributed to who I am today and who I'm becoming for tomorrow.

Lastly, but by no means least importantly, I thank you, the reader, for taking the time to read this book. You mean a lot to me.

ABOUT THE AUTHOR

Erik studied anthropology at UCLA and the University of Virginia, and used anthropology in business, helping a company grow from $7 million to over $100 million in ten years doing international business development. He also taught English as a second language for ten years in Japan, France, Thailand, and at universities in the USA. Erik uses entrepreneurial success formulas and motivational materials in business, but he's also pioneering their use in the field of education.

Erik has traveled to over 80 countries around the world and all 50 states in the USA. He also climbs mountains and has summited the highest peaks of nine countries and eight states. Experiences ranging from discussing philosophy at cafés in Paris to having a machine gun stuck in his mouth in Nigeria to living with a remote Indian tribe in the Amazon have forged in him a unique perspective that Erik uses to work through big life questions as well as small everyday decisions.

Erik is a writer, speaker, adventurer, entrepreneur, and educator who refuses to let others tell him what he can and cannot do. Erik's travels and intersections with people from around the world haven't been just a fun romp around the planet. They were a deep study of people, love, struggle, and ways of thinking that he relies on to tackle problems in school, business, and life.

Erik's most current ambitions are sharing the lessons he's learned with others and climbing mountains, which he says makes everyday challenges seem a lot easier.

Erik lives in Los Angeles with his wife and two boys.

CONNECT WITH ERIK

Erik is available for speaking, seminars, workshops, and interviews.

- Website: www.ErikSeversen.com
- Email: Erik@ErikSeversen.com
- Also find Erik on LinkedIn, Facebook, Instagram

Did you get your FREE GIFTS yet?

If you haven't gotten your free AFFECTION & RELATIONSHIP CALENDAR or your free GROWTH, GOALS, & ACCOUNTABILITY CALENDAR, Email Erik@ErikSeversen.com or go to www.ErikSeversen.com to get them right now.

Do you like a challenge?

THE EXTRAORDINARY HABITS CHALLENGE—Dare to Do It!

The Extraordinary Habits Challenge is a list of simple mental and physical habits that, when implemented into your routine, will greatly increase your energy, productivity, and sense of fulfillment. These habits will help you continue along the path of extraordinary success. Check it out right now at www.ErikSeversen.com.

DID YOU ENJOY THIS BOOK?

If you enjoyed reading this book, you can help me out by suggesting it to someone else you think might like it, and **please leave a positive review on Amazon**. This does a lot in helping others find the book. I thank you in advance for taking a few moments to do this for me.

***

You might also like Erik's first book, ***ORDINARY TO EXTRAORDINARY: Stories of Exotic Places and Remarkable People & How Belonging and Purpose Can Transform Your Life***. If you haven't read it yet, get your copy today at Amazon, Barnes & Noble, or wherever you shop for books.

***

THANK YOU

9 781732 336933